THE BEST OF

MANCHESTER UNITED

THE BEST OF
MANCHESTER UNITED

First published in the UK in 2007

Updated and reprinted in 2019

© G2 Entertainment Ltd 2019

www.G2ent.co.uk

Printed and bound printed in Europe

ISBN 978-1-782816-49-2

Contents

Aston:
John Aston Senior and John Aston Junior

BELOW John Aston, Senior

Born 23 September 1921, John Aston Senior began his Manchester United career on 18 September 1946 when he made his League debut against Chelsea at inside-forward. Matt Busby switched Aston's position to full-back, not only changing the number on his back, but also bringing out the best of his talent. Aston blossomed as a full-back bringing his expertise in pace and accuracy to a defensive position which he utilised to the full when he faced Stanley Matthews in the 1948 FA Cup Final.

During the difficult 1950-51 season, the versatile Aston was moved forward on several occasions giving him the opportunity to score 15 goals. He won 17 England caps before injury cut his career short. He then returned to Old Trafford as a youth team coach and, in 1970, became chief scout for the club, a position he held for two years.

Born the year after his father's debut on 28 June 1947, John Junior settled well at Old Trafford, turning professional in 1964. Not as glamorous as Best or Law, Aston Junior was often given a hard time by the home crowd who thought he lacked imagination, but he was nippy and direct, and he remained a loyal and committed player. Matt Busby was impressed and recognised his contribution to the team and he was a member of the 1967 Championship-winning side.

It was in the 1968 European Cup Final where Aston really shone. It became the pinnacle of his career as he repeatedly managed to pass Benfica's Adolfo on the left wing. He lost his first-team place after breaking his leg and was transferred to Luton Town for £30,000 in 1972.

ABOVE John Aston Jr in action

MIDDLE John Aston in a heading duel with Adolfo of Benfica in the European Cup Final at Wembley, 29 May 1968

He remained closely associated with the team and watched his son, John Aston Junior, also make his name at Old Trafford.

Atkinson

Ron Atkinson's first league job was as manager of Cambridge United in 1974. He had already gained experience with non-League clubs Witney Town and Kettering Town and went on to succeed Dave Sexton at Old Trafford in June 1981 after proving his worth with First Division West Bromwich Albion for three consecutive seasons.

Although United never finished lower than fourth in the League while he was at the helm, the Championship went to his home town, Liverpool, five seasons in a row. However, he won the FA Cup twice, claiming victory over Brighton in 1983 and Everton in 1985 with United setting a club record of ten consecutive League victories at the start of the 1985-86 season.

Renowned for spending large amounts on players, Atkinson only once paid more than £1 million for a player and that was for Bryan Robson who would be a loyal servant. The following season poor form cost Atkinson his job at Old Trafford and he returned to West Brom before moving to Atletico Madrid. He also man-

aged Sheffield Wednesday twice as well as Aston Villa and Coventry City. His successor at Old Trafford was a certain Alex Ferguson, who joined the club on 6 November 1986.

Beckham

David Beckham was born on 2 May 1975 and signed professionally for United in 1992 after joining as a trainee in 1991. He had come to United's attention after winning a Bobby Charlton skills competition at the age of 11. He made his first-team debut in September 1992 – coming on as a substitute at Brighton – but he had to wait a further two years for another chance and he made the most of it by scoring against Galatasaray in the European Cup.

He gained a regular place in midfield during 1995-96, scoring eight goals during 32 appearances and collecting an FA Cup winner's medal. The opening game against Wimbledon the following season was to mark the start of the David Beckham phenomenon when he scored from 57 yards in the dying minutes of the game.

Beckham made the transition from promising youngster to England's main creative force in just one season, making his debut under Glen Hoddle in September 1996 in Moldova. He enjoyed a momentous season and collected a second Championship medal and was voted the PFA's Young Player of the Year. Despite immense interest in his relationship with Victoria Adams (Posh Spice), Beckham continued to impress on the field, becoming United's top scorer during the 1997-98 season. But the World Cup in 1998 saw Beckham sent off after retaliation against an Argentinian player in a second-round match and many blamed him for England losing the game.

He returned from the World Cup to vitriolic abuse, but quickly knuckled down and proved wrong all those who thought his career in English football was over. He went on to captain the England side four years later and, despite going out in the quarter-finals to Brazil, the team returned home as heroes. Beckham enjoyed further

BELOW Beckham celebrates to the crowd after scoring a goal during the Premiership match against Everton, August 1997

ABOVE Beckham scores the opening goal during the league match between Villa and United at Villa Park, 2003

success at Old Trafford including the 1998-99 Treble before his departure to Real Madrid in June 2003.

After winning La Liga in his final season with the club he joined LA Galaxy in 2007, where he would help win the MSL Cup in 2011. His time in America also saw him have two loan spells with AC Milan, helping maintain the levels of fitness required to take him to 115 caps for his country, a record for an outfield player. Having been instrumental in helping London win the 2012 Olympic Games David was widely expected to be a member of the Team GB squad but was controversially omitted at the last stage.

Berbatov

Dimitar Berbatov is a classy centre-forward, pairing the ability to ruthlessly find the net inside the box with magical touches outside of it.

Berbatov started out at Bulgarian side CSKA Sofia where his talent quickly attracted the attention of Bundesliga club Bayer Leverkusen who made their move for the front man in January 2001. Although he was national team captain and Bulgarian Player of the Year in 2002, 2004, 2005 and 2007, he made a slow start to his time in Germany albeit regularly shining in the Champions League.

He was eventually lured to the Premier League when Tottenham signed him in July 2006 for a reported £10.9 million fee. He was an instant hit at White Hart Lane scoring his first competitive goal two minutes into his home League debut against Sheffield United. He went on to score 23 goals in his opening season, which he matched again in 2007-08.

After months of speculation linking him with a move to Old Trafford in the summer of 2008, Sir Alex Ferguson finally got his man on transfer deadline day with just minutes to go. Berbatov signed a four-year contract on 1 September 2008 for an undisclosed fee, with Fraizer Campbell heading to White Hart Lane on a season-long loan as part of the deal.

His tally of 48 goals in 108 League appearances helped United win two Premier Leagues, with Dimitar also picking up a winners medal in the Carling Cup in 2010. He also played in the 2009 Champions League final defeat against Barcelona and was omitted from the squad when the club reached the final again against the Spanish giants in 2011. Lack of first team football prompted a move to Fulham in August 2012.

BELOW Fabricio Coloccini of Newcastle United is unable to stop Dimitar Berbatov scoring

Best

On 16 August 1961, George Best signed as an apprentice for United and went on to become one of the most prolific professionals of all time. The 'Belfast Boy', born on 22 May 1946, went on to sign professionally in May 1963, making his League debut against West Bromwich Albion in September, but remained in the reserves until December that year when he scored in a 5-1 victory. He kept his place on the team and went on to play 466 League, Cup and European games, scoring 178 goals.

Although Best won 37 caps for Northern Ireland – he made his debut in April 1964 – he never actually played in the finals of a major tournament. Not only did he make a name for himself with his goalscoring, Best was renowned for taking on his opponents which was exciting for his fans. Women, particularly, took a shine to Best and football's popularity during the 1960s blossomed alongside his cult status. Best was also gifted at making space for his teammates, notably Bobby Charlton and Denis Law.

Nicknamed 'El Beatle' by the Portuguese after a European Cup match against Benfica in 1966, Best had become football's answer to the Liverpudlian pop idols with his entertaining football and rebel lifestyle. United won the Championship in 1967 and during the following season he enjoyed his greatest success, scoring 28 League goals and inspiring the team to become the first English club to win the European Cup. 1968 saw Best given the titles of Player of the Year, in both England and Northern Ireland, and European

Footballer of the Year.

Two seasons later, however, Best was involved in a number of clashes with referees, United started to go downhill, and late nights fuelled with alcohol added to the slippery slope. Matt Busby's retirement in 1969 seemed to mark the end for George Best. He was fined £100 and received a month's suspension for knocking the ball from the hands of a referee during a League Cup semi-final against Manchester City, During the 1968-69 season. His performance both on and off the pitch was becoming erratic, but he always remained a difficult opponent. At the end of the 1970 season he was sent off while playing for Northern Ireland for spitting and throwing mud at the referee.

Despite being the top United scorer in May 1971 with 18 goals, his relationship with the management team at United was suffering. In 1972, after failing to turn up to training, manager Frank O'Farrell dropped him, fined him two weeks' wages, gave him extra training and ordered him to return to digs. He then failed to report for Northern Ireland and in May 1972 he announced his retirement while in Spain. He did return but only scored four goals in 1972-73.

George Best played his last game for United on 1 January 1974 aged 27. He went on to play for a variety of clubs in England, Scotland and America but never again reached his outstanding form. He died in November 2005, aged 59, losing his battle with illnesses linked to alcoholism, and his death was mourned worldwide.

ABOVE George in action during the Division One match against Everton played at Old Trafford, in 1968

Brown

Wes Brown, born 13 October 1979, signed for United in November 1996 and despite injury setbacks, including a broken ankle, was set to become the team's strongest defender for many years. In his first full season his performances for the reserves and juniors – winning a Lancashire FA Youth Cup winner's medal and a Lancashire League Division One medal as well as the Denzil Haroun Young Player of the Year award – earned Brown his place on the first team, making his debut against Leeds in May 1998.

He is a solid, reliable defender who cemented his regular place when deputising for the injured Denis Irwin at full-back. His established international career at Under-18 and Under-21 levels ensured Brown a step up to the England team during the 1998-99 season, when he received his first cap under Kevin Keegan playing against Hungary in Budapest. Knee ligament injuries during 1999-2000 and his broken ankle at the end of the 2002-03 season were devastating for Brown, but he returned to full fitness and regained his place in the first team and earned himself an England recall.

Following the arrival of Vidic who struck up an understanding with Ferdinand, Wes Brown found opportunities limited, although he slotted in at right back when Gary Neville was side-lined with a long term injury during the 2007-08 season. Wes joined Sunderland in 2011, having made 232 League appearances for United.

Bruce

Steve Bruce is one of only 33 players to have appeared in more than 300 League games for United – he played a total of 410 times for the club. Bruce was born 31 December 1960 and began his career with Gillingham, having signed professionally for them in October 1978. The general consensus was that although he was committed, he lacked genuine talent – this turned out not to be true, as his illustrious career shows.

He was renowned for his determination and leadership which became an essential part of the most successful era in United's history. Bruce signed for United in December 1987 after a successful career at Norwich City who he joined in July 1984 on his departure from Priestfield. His grit and determination turned out to be just the qualities that United were looking for and he became their most reliable defender.

He had a seven-year partnership with Gary Pallister, whose pace and ball control complemented his own organisational skills. For a while, he was the club's penalty taker, which helped increase his scoring rate and in his eight and a half seasons he scored 51 times. He also scored the highest ever total for a defender during a single season in 1990-91 with 19 goals.

In 1992, Bruce took over the captaincy from Bryan Robson and in his four years as captain he lifted three Premiership trophies, the FA Cup and the League Cup, including the Double in 1993-94 and 1995-96. Bruce never got a full England call-up and left for Birmingham City (who he later managed) on a free transfer in 1996. He has also managed Sheffield United, Huddersfield, Crystal Palace, Wigan, Sunderland, Hull, Aston Villa, Sheffield Wednesday and Newcastle United.

ABOVE Bruce in action during a Premiership match against West Ham United at Upton Park, May 1995

RIGHT Buchan
during a Division
One match against
Leicester City at Old
Trafford, September
1980

Buchan

Another defender that made an impression at United, although earlier than Steve Bruce, was Martin Buchan, born 6 March 1949. After a successful career at Aberdeen, where he had been made captain aged 20, he led the team to a Scottish Cup victory. In 1971, he made his debut for Scotland – he went on to win 34 caps – and was voted Scottish Player of the Year.

Aberdeen decided to sell their young captain and Buchan chose United over the more successful Liverpool and Leeds clubs of the time. Frank O'Farrell paid £135,000 for Buchan who wasted no time in justifying the fee. Six months later, Tommy Docherty took over as manager, but despite relegation in 1974, once Buchan took over as captain of the team, United bounced back by winning the Second Division Championship in 1975. Then, in 1976, United reached the FA Cup Final but were bitterly disappointed when Southampton won by a single goal.

The following year saw United back in the Final with Liverpool. Despite the opposing side boasting Kevin Keegan, United won a memorable 2-1 victory.

Buchan was the first post-war player to captain both a Scottish and an English Cup-winning side. Persistent injuries led him to hang up his boots in 1983, and he now works for the Professional Footballers Association in Manchester.

Busby

The stadium at Old Trafford was a bombed-out wreck when Matt Busby arrived in October 1945. Initially offered a three-year contract by Chairman James Gibson, Busby argued for a term of five years. He wanted to realise his vision which he knew would take time and patience. He also demanded to be given the authority to appoint his own staff and act on his own judgement, asking for both power and responsibility.

The first thing Busby did was to put Jimmy Murphy in charge of the reserve team and heavily involve him with the youth project. Their working partnership was to last for almost 30 years. One by one, the United players returned from the war, most of whom had not seen more than one season of first-team action. All were keen to learn from Busby, who set about preparing his team with a number of positional changes, the results of which were to prove invaluable.

Johnny Carey found his niche at full-back, while John Aston Senior discovered his forte as a defender. Henry

ABOVE Sir Matt Busby, 1991

Cockburn became a wing-half.

and Jimmy Delaney transferred from Celtic to form the 'famous five' in the forwards alongside Pearson, Rowley, Mitten and Morris. United ended the 1946-47 season as runners-up in the League. In 1948 they won the FA Cup, beating Blackpool 4-2 to become the first of three great teams.

Busby, who was knighted in 1968 and given the freedom of the City of Manchester, died in 1994. His statue stands outside Old Trafford in Sir Matt Busby Way.

Busby Babes

Matt Busby assumed managerial control of United mid-season in October 1945. His vision was to use the youth development programme to produce the club's own players and it was in November 1951, after journalist Tom Jackson of the *Manchester Evening News* watched Jackie Blanchflower and Roger Byrne, aged 18 and 21, make their debut against Liverpool at Anfield, that he nicknamed them the 'United Babes'. Not long after, Busby was joined to the name and the 'Busby Babes' were born.

The Busby Babes roll-call included Johnny Berry, Jackie Blanchflower, Roger Byrne, Bobby Charlton, Eddie Colman, Duncan Edwards, Mark Jones, Wilf McGuinness, David Pegg, Albert Scanlon, Tommy Taylor, Dennis Viollet, Liam Whelan and Ray Wood. Although not all the Babes had grown up through the youth programme, they were part of the phenomenon that hit English football during the 1950s.

The reign of the Busby Babes was only brought to an end by the Munich air disaster in which eight members of the team were killed. Busby strove to create a youth scheme that included four or five teams on each tier of the programme. The foundations were already in place with the Manchester United Junior Athletic Club having been formed in 1938 by the then secretary Walter Crickmer and chairman James Gibson.

The MUJAC, which had encouraged the likes of John Aston Senior, set the model that Busby was to develop and it was with the experience of chief scouts Louis Rocca and his successor Joe Armstrong that helped the programme achieve success. The aim was to seek out talented young players and

enhance their abilities by giving them the chance to train with professional trainers and coaches.

Armstrong was particularly adept at persuading anxious parents that their talented young sons would do well at United. It was his foresight to see the potential in schoolboy players, such as Charlton and Edwards, that gave the club the young talent it needed. Attendances began to grow at youth games as word about the success and talent of the team spread and, in 1953, Matt Busby took his young team to Zurich to compete in the International Youth Cup. Despite the youth of the team they were incredibly mature players and Matt Busby is said to have disliked the nickname.

The Babes were primed to take over the first team but the transition was gradual and it was not until the mid-1950s that all elements Busby thought were necessary were in place. The team beat the League Champions Chelsea in November 1955 and it was from then on that the team made its ascent, going on to win the League Cup in 1957, the FA Cup in 1956 and 1957 and the Charity Shield. The last time the Busby Babes lined up together on the pitch was 5 February 1958 in Belgrade.

LEFT Duncan Edwards throwing in the ball, 1957

BELOW Roger Byrne
clears the ball

Byrne

Roger Byrne, born 8 February 1929, was possibly one of Matt Busby's most astute signings for United. Part of the youth programme, Byrne played at wing-half, inside-forward and then wing again in both the 'A' team and the Reserves, but on his first-team debut in November 1951 he played at left-back. He made 24 appearances in his first season, making a reputation for himself during the latter half going back to his familiar role as left-wing, scoring seven times and helping United to their first Championship in 41 seasons.

In October 1952 Byrne asked for a transfer, unhappy with his place on the wing. Busby immediately reinstated him to the position of left-back and he played for the remainder of the season in his favoured position. When Johnny Carey decided to retire in May 1953 aged 34, Allenby Chilton stood in as captain, but the real potential lay with Byrne, who assumed the role in February 1954. Busby had decided by this time it was necessary to bring more young blood into the side and Byrne became mentor to the young Busby Babes.

Despite his tendency to tell his manager when he did not like something, Busby and Byrne held each other in high regard and Busby liked his captain's leadership qualities. In 1954 he was picked to play for England against Scotland and it turned out to be the first of 33 consecutive caps for his country, despite never scoring and even missing two penalties against Brazil and Yugoslavia. Roger Byrne won three Championship winner's medals with United before his death in Munich.

Cantona

Alex Ferguson described Eric Cantona as "...the catalyst for the Championships. He brought a vision that we did not have before. Although I thought we were getting there, Cantona certainly accelerated it. He was an absolutely phenomenal player."

In just over four years at United, Cantona was an essential part of the club winning the League Championship four times. This was exceptional considering that the club had not won it for 26 years. Cantona, like George Best, was worshipped by the fans who called him 'the King', or 'God'. Cantona, however, remained a man of mystery. He had a love of poetry, art and philosophy that didn't somehow fit with the perception of a Premiership footballer. He was also an unconventional striker who preferred to drop off deep and play just behind the forward line. He had the rare talent of being able to create space and time for himself.

Cantona was born in Paris on 24 May 1966 and after spells at various clubs in France signed for Leeds in February 1992, joining United in November that year for £1 million. He quickly settled into his new team and signs of his influence were seen with a 4-1 victory over Tottenham in January 1993 – United only lost one of 23 games in which he played dur-

ABOVE Cantona in action during the FA Premiership match between Manchester United and Middlesbrough at Old Trafford, October 1995

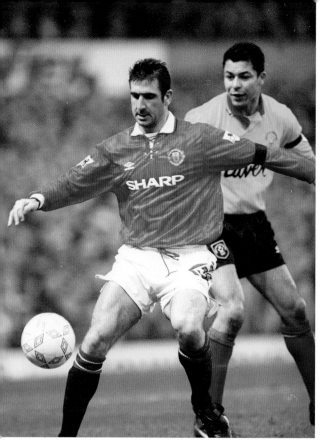

ing 1992-93. Six months after signing Cantona, the club were Champions. In his first full season, United won their first ever Double and he became the first foreigner to ever be voted PFA Player of the Year.

A few years later, however, trouble loomed and, after attacking a Crystal Palace fan who was verbally abusing him in January 1995, Cantona was sentenced to two weeks' imprisonment. This was reduced on appeal to 120 hours' community service, but without Cantona (banned for eight months), United failed in their defence of the Double and finished as runners-up in both the League and the FA Cup.

In October 1995, Cantona returned and managed to keep his temper under control. He was determined that United would reclaim both titles. The closest challenger at the time was Newcastle, but they were no contest for United with Cantona on the pitch. The double Double was won in 1996 and he redeemed himself.

The following season Cantona captained the side to a fourth Premiership title. However, he took United's failure to reach the European Cup Final particularly badly and he decided to retire from football a week after lifting the Premiership trophy. Of the 19 penalties that he took for United, Cantona only missed two. He scored 80 League and Cup goals, 14 with his head.

Carey

John Joseph Carey, born 23 February 1919, used his brains as well as his brawn during his spell at United using a style which completely changed the way full-backs play. On a visit to Dublin, long-time chief scout, Louis Rocca, was impressed by his thoughtful way on the pitch and Rocca signed the young Irishman for £250. He described him later as the best, cheapest and most successful signing he ever made. Carey went on to captain one of England's greatest teams as well as setting a record by playing for both the Republic of Ireland and Northern Ireland.

In his time at United, Carey played 344 times and scored 18 goals from his position as full-back. He made his debut for the club in September 1937 at the age of 18, playing inside-forward, and helped the club to be promoted from the Second Division. It was also during this year that he won his first international cap for the Republic of Ireland. Joining the British Army in 1939, he served in North Africa and Italy. During this time he was fortunate to play football and made guest appearances for several Italian clubs.

On his return from World War II, Matt Busby had been newly installed as United's manager. Carey's position as inside-forward was taken by Pearson and Busby's decision to play him as full-back was pure luck. The United board were not impressed by the decision as Carey did not fit the description of a big, brawny lad who could tackle hard and Busby nearly lost his job. Busby's determination to stick to his guns, however, brought great rewards for the club. Carey became captain and found his niche enabling him to organise the defence and attack from deep down the pitch. Success in the League, however, eluded the team.

This changed in 1948 when the team won the FA Cup against Blackpool. A year later Carey captained the Republic of Ireland team when they became the first foreign team to beat England on their own soil. He retired in 1953 and went on to coach and manage Blackburn Rovers.

ABOVE John Carey, one of United's celebrated Irishmen, was a star of the early postwar era

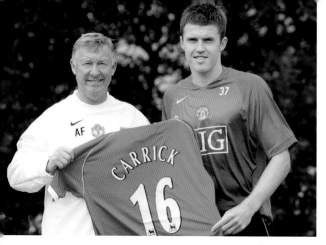

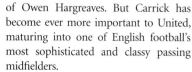

Carrick

Michael Carrick had his detractors at the start of his United career – with some grumblings about his £18 million transfer fee – but he proved his worth with his consistency and stabilizing influence in midfield.

Even after his debut in the 2006-07 season, in which he carved out a formidable partnership with Paul Scholes as the Reds reclaimed the title, some people predicted he'd slip down the pecking order after the arrival of Owen Hargreaves. But Carrick has become ever more important to United, maturing into one of English football's most sophisticated and classy passing midfielders.

The first of Carrick's five League titles with United was also the first major honour of his professional career having played for West Ham and Spurs while they were going through barren spells.

When he first joined United he was encouraged by Sir Alex Ferguson to push forward and eventually weighed in with six strikes from midfield in 2006-07. Indeed his second goal, at home to Reading in the FA Cup, was shortlisted for the club's Goal of the Season award (won by a Scholes screamer away to Villa).

Carrick may have only scored three goals in 2007-08 but his all round contribution to the cause could not be questioned as the Reds were crowned Champions of England and Europe.

He went on to help the club win their 20th League title (a new record) and reach two further Champions League finals, although both were lost to Barcelona.

Michael retired from playing in 2018 after 464 appearances for United and quickly became an integral part of the club's coaching staff.

Champions League

Having been the first English club to win the European Cup in 1968, by the time United next won the League title 25 years later the competition had been expanded and renamed the Champions League. United's return to Europe's flag-ship competition in 1993-94 saw them ease past Honved before going out on the away goal rule to Galatasaray. The following year saw the introduction of the group stage and, despite gaining revenge on Galatasaray with a 4-0 home victory, United failed to progress to the second round after suffering defeats at Barcelona and IFK Gothenburg.

Despite losing three of the six group matches in 1996-97, United managed to

BELOW Ole Gunnar Solskjaer celebrates scoring the second goal during the Champions League Final against Bayern Munich in the Nou Camp, 1999

scrape through to the quarter-final where a 4-0 home display against Porto, coupled with a goal-less draw in the return, saw them line up a semi-final they lost to eventual Champions Borussia Dortmund.

Many thought 1998 would prove to be United's year as it would be 40 years on from Munich and the 30th anniversary of their previous triumph. Five victories in their group games boded well, but Monaco claimed a semi-final berth on away goals.

United were forced to suffer the ignominy of the qualifying round the following year before they could embark on an unbeaten run through the group stage. They were to face Italian opponents in both the quarter and semi-final games in Inter Milan and Juventus, but held their nerves to book their place in the Final in Barcelona. Bayern Munich took a

sixth-minute lead in the Final and it took two last-gasp goals by substitutes Teddy Sheringham and Ole Gunnar Solksjaer to bring the trophy back to Old Trafford on what would have been Sir Matt Busby's 90th birthday.

United have competed for 15 consecutive seasons up to 2010-11 – a record – and claimed their third European crown in 2008. After Ronaldo had headed United into the lead against Chelsea in Moscow, Fergie's side could have gone in at half-time three goals to the good, had Tevez taken his chances. Lampard equalised shortly before the interval, and extra time failed to separate the teams. Misses by Ronaldo and Terry in the penalty shoot-out led to sudden death and, when Van Der Sar saved from Anelka, the trophy was heading for Old Trafford.

They nearly became the first side to retain the trophy when they were back in the final the following year, when they lost to Barcelona, falling to goals from Eto'o and Messi.

United were drawn against Rangers, Valencia and Bursaspor in the group stages of the 2010-11 Champions League. In 2011 the same two sides again reached the final, this time at Wembley, where Barcelona were to win 3-1.

Charity / Community Shield

ABOVE Celebrations following victory in the 2007 Community Shield

Manchester United has won a record 20 FA Charity Shield matches since its inception in 1908 when Football League Champions United emerged victorious over Southern League Champions Queen's Park Rangers in a Stamford Bridge replay. They have also shared the Shield on four occasions when the match ended in a draw before the introduction of penalty shoot-outs.

United participated in the highest-scoring Shield match when they beat Swindon Town 8-4 in 1911. While Alex Stepney was embarrassed when Tottenham goalkeeper Pat Jennings scored against him with a long kick from his own penalty area at Old Trafford in 1967 in a match that finished 3-3.

In the 1990s, Manchester United appeared in no fewer than seven Shield matches – winning four (including two on penalties, against Arsenal in 1993 and Chelsea in 1997), drawing one and losing two. The Charity Shield was renamed the FA Community Shield in 2001 and United have continued their love affair with a further six victories, taking their overall tally to 16 outright victories and four shared.

Their victory over Wigan in the 2013/14 season curtain raiser was David Moyes only trophy during his short term as manager.

The Community Shield was won once more in 2016 when cup winners United overcame Premier League title winners Leicester.

Charlton

Football was in Bobby Charlton's blood. His mother came from the Milburn soccer family in the northeast with four brothers playing professionally, while her cousin was the legendary Newcastle United centre-forward Jackie Milburn. Not surprisingly two of her sons took up the game and Jack played for Leeds and England.

Born 11 October 1937 near Newcastle, Bobby Charlton joined United's ground staff in June 1953. As a schoolboy player, it was rumoured that at least 18 clubs wanted to sign him, but he made a promise to join United. His early years saw him score regularly as a reserve, and finally make his debut in October 1956 scoring two goals. He was dropped for the next game to make way for the recently recovered Tommy Taylor.

There was much competition as the Busby Babes started to grow in number and Charlton was only picked to play when various members of the team were injured, notably, Billy Whelan, Taylor or Dennis Viollet. By the end of 1956-57 he was playing more regularly however. With exemplary behaviour both on and off the pitch, Charlton was set to do well with his exceptional eye for the goal. The emerging Babes side enjoyed Championship success with the help of ten goals scored by Charlton during the 1956-57 season. Also at this time he played in the FA Cup team and scored during the semi-final, going on to play in the Final against Aston Villa.

Success eluded the team, but undeterred, Charlton went on to make his European Cup debut against Real Madrid. When their plane crashed at Munich airport on 6 February 1958, eight United players were killed. Charlton escaped serious injury having been dragged unconscious from the wreckage by goalkeeper Harry Gregg.

In the following month after the disaster, Charlton returned to action in the FA Cup sixth round. The team reached the Final, but lost to Bolton. Charlton remained a constant player for Busby, while other players came and went.

The aftermath of the accident was a difficult time for all at Old Trafford and Matt Busby was often in despair. He found in Charlton a great source of inspiration. Charlton, meanwhile, was committed to playing for his club. He made his England debut in April 1958 against Scotland at Hampden Park. He played mostly left-wing and took part in 38 League games, scoring 28 goals, but he didn't feel involved enough. He found his niche in midfield in 1964 where he was able to unleash his creative skills and contribute greatly to Championship success.

Charlton was instrumental in helping England to the World Cup Final in 1966, belting two fine goals past the Portuguese keeper in an earlier game. England won the World Cup in spectacular fashion and Charlton was then voted Footballer of the Year, European Footballer of the Year and Model Player by the referees. In 1968, at the pinnacle of his career, he helped

United to their European Cup triumph over Benfica at Wembley.

Bobby Charlton held the record for most appearances for the club (753 in all competitions) until this was smashed by Ryan Giggs (who has played nearly 1000 games) although he is still the highest goal-scorer with 247 goals. Having already been awarded an OBE, and a CBE, he was knighted for his services to football in 1994 and remains a legendary figurehead at the club – arguably the most respected player in its history.

ABOVE Bobby Charlton in action during a match

Coppell

Born 9 July 1955 in Liverpool, Steve Coppell signed for United in 1975. He had slick ball skills that made him a natural choice for both United and England until injury halted his playing career in 1983.

BELOW Coppell motivates his team-mates during a match, September 1980

While studying at Liverpool University, Coppell had joined Third Division Tranmere Rovers, but United's manager, Tommy Docherty spotted his talent and he moved to Old Trafford in early 1975, taking over from winger Willie Morgan. Although his first season ended in losing to Second Division Southampton in the FA Cup Final, United returned to Wembley in May 1977 to defeat Liverpool 2-1, where Coppell picked up the only winner's medal of his career.

In 1981, during an England game, Coppell seriously injured his knee in a tackle with Josef Roth of Hungary. This led to three operations from which he never fully recovered and 14 months later, aged just 28, he was forced to retire from playing professional football. He had played 206 consecutive League games between 1977 and 1981, a United record. He later went on to manage Crystal Palace, Manchester City, Brighton and Reading where he resigned after the final match of the season in 2009. He became manager of Bristol City in April 2010 but resigned four months later. He was formerly Director of Football at Crawley Town and Portsmouth for short spells but has yet to make a managerial comeback in the UK

Crerand

Renowned for being a tough midfielder, Pat Crerand (born 19 March 1939) signed for United in 1962. He had joined Glasgow Celtic in 1957 at the age of 18. Three months after arriving at Old Trafford, Crerand won the first of many medals including an FA Cup winner's medal against Leicester City in 1963. He quickly established himself as one of United's most constructive midfielders and was known for being an aggressive tackler.

His vision and ability to send the ball long made up for his lack of goals and he became a key member of the United side that won the League Championship in 1965 and 1967 and the European Cup in 1968. Along with Bobby Charlton and Nobby Stiles, Crerand formed one of United's finest ever midfield trios. He had an unquestionable loyalty to Matt Busby and the club and was arguably sometimes too committed, allowing his temper to get the better of him. In a match against Partizan Belgrade in 1966 he was sent off for fighting, but two years later won the European Cup with United against Benfica at Wembley.

During the 1971-72 season, he retired from playing and for a brief time was assistant manager to Tommy Docherty, before becoming manager of Northampton Town in 1976. Crerand's unflinching support for the club and a local radio commentator's job still earn him high regard with supporters.

BELOW Crerand warming up before a game, January 1968

De Gea

Despite a dodgy start at United, the youthful-looking keeper has repaid faith that Sir Alex Ferguson showed in him by paying a British record fee of £17.8 million to bring him to the club.

A product of Atletico Madrid's academy, the tall athletic glovesman progressed quickly through the youth ranks and made his first-team debut against FC Porto in the Champions League on 30 September 2009 - and thereafter he never looked back.

De Gea capped his maiden campaign in Atletico's first team by playing a major role in winning the UEFA Europa League - the club's first major European trophy in almost 50 year – and it wasn't long before the Reds' then goalkeeping coach Eric Steele was seen scouting the youngster.

In June 2011, he was signed to replace the retiring Edwin van der Sar at Old Trafford. Despite his tender years (he is still in his mid 20s), De Gea enjoyed a largely successful first campaign in Manchester although he dropped the occasional clanger which the media pounced on.

Unfortunately, his first season ended with title heartbreak on the final day but the experience stood him in good stead during the 2012-13 campaign when, along with his team-mates, the Barclays Premier League title was reclaimed at a canter.

De Gea was a standout figure throughout his second season, earning a place in the prestigious PFA Team of the Year, and now has nearly 200 appearances under his belt for the Reds.

He was also the team's best player in the 2013-14 and 2014-15 seasons (prompting overtures from Real Madrid where he looks to be heading) and his next personal target is to become the first choice keeper for the national side, whom he has captained at Under 21s, ousting Casillas in the process.

Derbies

The first ever Manchester derby took place on 3 October 1891 when Newton Heath beat Ardwick 5-1 in an FA Cup first round qualifier. There have since been more than 150 meetings between the two local rivals with the red half of Manchester holding the upper hand as the tables below show.

In recent times the rivalry has moved up a notch or two, with City winning 6-1 at Old Trafford and then 1-0 at the Etihad Stadium during the 2011-12 season, on their way to winning the title at United's expense on goal difference! City's elevation has also seen the two clubs meet in considerably more meaningful matches, with City winning an FA Cup semi final at Wembley 1-0 in April 2011

and United winning a thrilling FA Community Shield match at the same venue 3-2 four months later.

The first Manchester Derby of the 2013-14 season was won by City 4-1 at the Etihad Stadium. It was the first time in 26 years that the Derby had been contested by two new managers: Manuel Pellegrini for City and David Moyes for United. One of them lasted to the end of the season and won the Premier League; one of them didn't!

ABOVE The blue and red halves of Manchester are seperated by stewards and police

Competition	City Wins	Draws	United Wins
League	47	51	62
League Cup	3	1	3
FA Cup	3	0	5
Community Shield	0	0	2
Total	**53**	**52**	**72**

*Figures to end of 2018-19 season

ABOVE Tommy Docherty, the Manchester United manager from 1972 to 1977

Docherty

Before his move to Manchester United in December 1972, Tommy Docherty was a player with Preston and Arsenal, a Scottish international and the manager of Scotland.

Known as 'The Doc', he brought new players to Old Trafford and avoided relegation but this proved to be short-lived, because in April 1974 United were relegated to the Second Division for the first time since 1937. They were Second Division Champions in 1975 and Docherty took his team to the 1976 FA Cup Final where they were beaten by Southampton. Undeterred, United fought back under Docherty's leadership and beat Liverpool 2-1 the following season to claim the trophy.

This was to be Docherty's last match in charge as, when his affair with the club physiotherapist's wife was revealed on 3 June 1977, he lost his job. He continued his career and went on to manage Chelsea, QPR three times, Aston Villa, Rotherham, FC Porto, Derby County, Preston and Wolverhampton Wanderers, ending his career with a short spell in Australia and as manager of non-League Altrincham.

Double

Considering only three teams had previously managed to complete the Double of League title and FA Cup in the 20th century (Tottenham Hotspur in 1961, Arsenal in 1971 and Liverpool in 1986), the fact that Manchester United achieved this feat twice in three seasons underlines their dominance of the domestic game in the 1990s.

Following the capture of their first League title for more than a quarter of a century, United went into the 1993-94 season on a high. By the end of March, they had lost just two League games – both home and away to Chelsea – and would finish the season by suffering just two more defeats to finish with a then-record Premiership points tally of 92. The FA Cup Final saw a 4-0 demolition of Chelsea with Cantona netting two penalties. Sadly, Sir Matt Busby passed away on 20 January so would never see his beloved United register their first Double.

United claimed their second Double in 1995-96, this time losing six games en route to the Premiership title although they remained unbeaten at Old Trafford.

Chelsea were the victims in the semi-final this year and it fell to Cantona to score the only goal of the FA Cup Final against Liverpool. United can also claim two other doubles, having won the Premier League and Champions League in 2007-08 and the Premier League and Carling Cup in 2009-10.

LEFT United players celebrate victory after the FA Cup Final match against Newcastle United where they completed the Double for the third time in six years, May 1999

Edwards

Born 1 October 1936, Duncan Edwards became the youngest ever player in the First Division at the age of just 16. He made his international debut aged 18 for England in the 7-2 victory over Scotland in April 1955, becoming the youngest international player of the 20th century. It is argued that Edwards was the best United player of all time.

By the time of his death, aged 21, in the Munich tragedy, he had earned the nickname 'manboy' because he helped United to win the Youth Cup in the same month that he made his international debut. He won three Youth Cups, two League titles and an FA Cup Finalist's medal.

What made Edwards stand out initially was his size. At 15 he had looked like a giant and played like a man in the opinion of Matt Busby. But he combined awesome power with a lighter touch, he could kill the ball dead and

dribble as well as unleashing an accurate 50-yard pass. Edwards was unassuming and liked by his team-mates who just accepted that he could achieve more physically than they could. As left-back, he usually wore the number six shirt, but he was gifted enough to play virtually anywhere on the pitch.

The Busby Babes were a talented bunch, but Edwards was a natural. For 15 days after the Munich crash, he defied chronic kidney damage, a collapsed lung, a broken pelvis and ribs as well as a smashed right thigh before his death on 21 February 1958. Sir Bobby Charlton had the ultimate praise for his former team-mate: "The best player I've ever seen, the best footballer I've ever played with for United or England, and the only player who ever made me feel inferior."

European Cup

United's first outing in the European Cup took place on 12 September 1956 when they beat Anderlecht 2-0 away. In the return leg at Maine Road, the home side registered their record European victory with a 10-0 rout. Their run would take them to the semi-final where they lost to holders Real Madrid.

The 1957-58 season saw United again qualify to compete against Europe's elite. This was made more poignant, however, by the Munich air disaster which had occurred as the team were returning home from their victorious quarter-final second leg clash against Red Star Belgrade. The team that beat AC Milan 2-1 in the home leg but lost 4-0 in the San Siro contained just four of the players (Gregg, Foulkes, Morgans and Viollet) whose efforts had got United this far.

It would take until 1965-66 for United to again qualify. They got to the semi-final once more, having defeated the mighty Benfica 8-3 on aggregate in the quarter-final with George Best outshining the newly-crowned European Footballer of the Year Eusebio. But United went out at the hands of Partizan Belgrade.

Their next attempt to claim Europe's top club prize would be successful, however, as Hibernian Malta, Sarajevo and Gornik Zabrze were despatched en route to a semi-final showdown with Real Madrid. Taking a slender 1-0 lead to the Bernabeu, United battled out a 3-3 draw to earn themselves a place in the Final against Benfica. Bobby Charlton (apart from Foulkes, the only Munich survivor in the side) opened the scoring in the second half before Jaime Graca equalised for the Portuguese. Extra time saw three goals from George Best, 19-year-old birthday boy Brian Kidd and a second for Charlton bring the trophy back to England for the first time.

The attempt to retain the trophy began well with a 10-2 aggregate mauling of Irish side Waterford and victories against Anderlecht and Rapid Vienna but AC Milan prevailed.

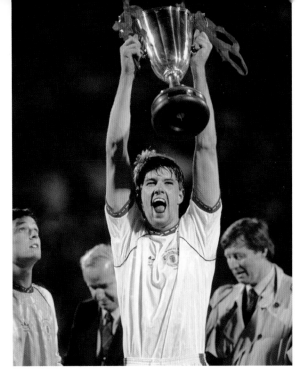

European Cup Winners' Cup

United's first foray into the European Cup Winners' Cup came in 1963-64 when they overcame Willem II and Tottenham Hotspur before beating Sporting Lisbon 4-1 at Old Trafford and then losing 5-0 in Portugal to exit the competition. More than a decade would pass before United once again graced the competition, this time registering a victory over St Etienne. They came away from Porto with a 4-0 deficit that they failed to claw back in the return leg, winning 5-2 with goals from Steve Coppell (2) and Jimmy Nicholl and a brace of own goals.

Juventus halted their progress in 1983-84, with United having disposed of Dukla Prague, Spartak Varna and Barcelona in previous rounds. United finally claimed this trophy on 15 May 1991. Having knocked out Pecsi Munkas, Wrexham, Montpellier and Legia Warsaw on their way to the Final, they now came up against Barcelona in Rotterdam. Mark Hughes scored twice in the 2-1 victory against his former club.

United also went on to compete in the European Super Cup as a result and a Brian McClair goal at Old Trafford against Red Star Belgrade gave Alex Ferguson a second European trophy in six months. United's attempt to defend their Cup Winners' Cup title ended with a second-round 4-1 aggregate loss at the hands of Atletico Madrid.

European Footballer of the Year

That three Manchester United players won the European Footballer of the Year trophy in the space of five years in the 1960s showed that this was no ordinary era for the team and that Law, Charlton and Best were very special talents.

Law was the first of the trio to be honoured after scoring 46 goals in 40 League and Cup games during the 1963-64 season; Charlton was given both the domestic and continental accolade in 1965-66 in helping England to World Cup glory; while Best won the award in 1968 after helping to bring the European Cup to Old Trafford.

The latest Red recipient of the Ballon d'Or, as it is commonly called, is Cristiano Ronaldo who won the award in 2008 again, like Best, after helping United win the European Cup.

Evra

Originally an attacker, Evra's career began to take off when he was switched to the defence, where his pace, positioning and awareness would enable him to become one of the best full backs in the modern game.

Born in Dakar in Senegal on 15 May 1981, he began his career with local club Les Ulis but moved to Italy to play for Masala as a youngster. He moved to France in 2000 to join Nice, where he made the switch to full back and quickly became a player to watch, signing for Monaco in 2002. A French League winner in 2003 he would also help the club reach the final of the Champions League in 2004. In January 2006 United beat of fierce competition to bring him to Old Trafford, signing a player who was equally at home on the left side of midfield as he was in the back four.

At the end of the season he had helped the club win the League title, but United fans did not see the best of him until the following campaign. With a proper United pre-season under his belt, he became one of the mainstays of a side that would go on to lift the Champions League.

Evra added to his tally of honours with a total of five League titles, three League Cups and the aforementioned Champions League. After 379 appearances for the Reds, he was reluctant to leave United for Juventus in July 2014 although he promptly helped the club win the Serie A title and reach the Champions' League Final in his first year.

Evra was also a regular for France until as captain he led a players' mutiny during the 2010 tournament and was exiled from the national side although has since returned to win more than 60 caps for his country.

FA Cup

Manchester United have won the FA Cup 12 times and appeared in 20 finals. Indeed, they are the only club to have appeared in a Final in every decade since the war.

Their debut in the competition ended in a 6-1 first round drubbing at the hands of holders Preston in 1890. Their first taste of success came in 1909 when a Billy Meredith-inspired United emerged victorious with Sandy Turnbull scoring the only goal of the game. It would be almost 40 years before United again graced the Final, this time a 4-2 victory over Blackpool giving Matt Busby his first trophy in 1948.

The late 1950s will be remembered with United finishing twice as runners-up. The first time, in 1957, saw the club hoping to complete the first Double of the century, but a clash with Villa's Peter McParland left keeper Ray Wood

ABOVE Cristiano Ronaldo and Glen Johnson of Portsmouth battle for the ball during the FA Cup quarter-final, 2008

with concussion and a fractured cheekbone. Jackie Blanchflower stood in as his deputy (these were the days before substitutes) but conceded twice as Villa ran out 2-1 winners. The following year, the remnants of the pre-Munich side reached the Final only to lose 2-0 to Bolton Wanderers as Nat Lofthouse bundled Harry Gregg into the net for a controversial goal.

There was only one appearance in the 1960s, a 3-1 win over Leicester City in 1963 before a shock defeat at the hands of Second Division Southampton in 1976. United made amends the following year when they disposed of Liverpool 2-1 with goals from Stuart Pearson and Jimmy Greenhoff. Arsenal won the 1979 Final with a dramatic late Alan Sunderland goal taking the spoils

just a minute after Sammy McIlroy had brought United level.

Two Finals in three years followed, with United overcoming relegated Brighton 4-0 in the 1983 replay after the two sides had played out a 2-2 thriller and dealing Everton's Double hopes a fatal blow two years later. Crystal Palace were the opposition in 1990 when, again after a replay, Alex Ferguson claimed his first trophy as Manchester United manager.

A hat-trick of Final appearances began in 1994 with a 4-0 victory over Chelsea and a 1-0 win over Liverpool sandwiching a 1-0 defeat against Everton. The second leg of the Treble was secured in 1999 with a 2-0 victory over Newcastle United before two more back-to-back appearances.

The 2004 victory over Millwall provided scant compensation for the surrender of the Premiership title to Arsenal. The following year saw the Old Trafford club finish the season empty-handed with Chelsea taking the title and Arsenal claiming the Cup Final on penalties after United had dominated the match. United reasserted their Cup pedigree by reaching the first Final at the new Wembley in 2007 which they lost by a single goal to Chelsea. They also lost in 2018, 1-0 to Chelsea - two years after lifting the trophy by beating Crystal Palace 2-1 in the final.

Famous Fans

The list of celebrity fans of Manchester United is endless but they include, from the music world: Victoria Beckham (former Spice Girl and wife of David), Richard Ashcroft (the Verve), Ian Brown (the Stone Roses), Tim Burgess (the Charlatans), Mick Hucknall (Simply Red), Kym Marsh and opera singer Russell Watson.

Former England cricket captain Michael Atherton and snooker player John Virgo (*Big Break*) are two of the many sports stars to follow the Red Devils, as do television personalities Eamonn Holmes (former GMTV presenter), Terry Christian (*The Word*), comedian Steve Coogan (*Alan Partridge*), Angus Deayton (the former *Have I Got News For You* host), Patrick Kielty (the Irish comedian who fronted *Fame Academy*

ABOVE Opera singer Russell Watson sings before the FA Cup Final, 2002

LEFT TV news presenter Eamonn Holmes is a famous fan

and *Celebrity Love Island*), TV chef Gary Rhodes and former weather girl turned presenter Ulrika Jonsson. They also attract a multitude of soapstars including *Emmerdale's* Mark Charnock (Marlon Dingle) and Lisa Riley (Mandy Dingle), *Coronation Street's* Michael Le Vell (Kevin Webster) and Sean Wilson (Martin Platt), *EastEnders'* Steve McFadden (Phil Mitchell) and *Dream Team's* Terry Kiely (Fletch) to name a few. Other actors who have proclaimed their loyalty to Old Trafford include James Nesbitt (*Cold Feet* and the voice of *Tractor Tom*) and Christopher Eccleston (the former *Dr Who*).

FA Premiership

Having failed to win the first Division title between 1967 and 1992, the inception of the Premier League in 1992-93 saw United claim the trophy at the first attempt and retain it the following year. The final day of the 1995 season arrived with United being in a position to claim a hat-trick of trophies if they beat West Ham United and Blackburn failed to beat Liverpool. As it turned out, Blackburn lost at Anfield but United could only manage a 1-1 draw at Upton Park so the title went to Ewood Park.

With Eric Cantona reinstated to the side following his eight-month ban, United began to reel in Kevin Keegan's Newcastle United side that had amassed a seemingly unassailable lead at the top of the Premiership. A 1-0 victory at St James' Park in March 1997 brought the gap to one point and proved a turning point as the Magpies finished the season in second place, four points adrift.

United finished second to Arsenal in 1997-98 but then went on to win three consecutive Premierships before their dominance faded.

Chelsea again dominated the 2006 campaign but United went on to complete another hat-trick of Premier League wins on May 16 2009, when they secured their 11th Premier League title – and 18th League title overall – following a 0-0 draw at home to Arsenal.

United finished second to Arsenal on 1997-98 but then went on to assert their dominance, winning three consecutive titles, the first time this had been achieved in the Premier League (and only the third time overall). After battling the twin London threat from Chelsea and Arsenal for three years, United were back on top in 2007 and again struck up three consecutive title wins.

In 2011 United reclaimed the title from Chelsea and in so doing finally overtook Liverpool's tally of title victories, registering their nineteenth championship. In Sir Alex Fergsuon's final season in charge, United clinched their 20th title in 2013 – a fitting send-off to the man who had a burning ambition to win more Premierships than any other team.

BELOW Manchester United celebrate after winning the Premier League, 2009

ABOVE Rio Ferdinand clears as AS Roma forward Mirko Vucinic looks on during their Champions League match, April 2008

Ferdinand

After his talents as an accomplished defender in the 2002 World Cup were made evident, Alex Ferguson decided that Rio Ferdinand (born 7 November 1978) was just what United needed to sort out their shaky defence. He was transferred from West Ham United for the record fee for a defender of £30 million and signed for United in July 2002.

Ferdinand is renowned for his calm ability on the ball, his talent for maintaining great pace and his aerial flair. Armed with good organisational skills and his talent to anticipate the game, Ferdinand has established himself as one of the world's top defenders. He only really found his feet at United towards the end of his first season, after injury and lack of form hampered his efforts at the start, and he helped United win their 15th League title.

In September 2003, Ferdinand missed a routine drugs test and despite appealing was banned for eight months in January 2004. He was the team's defensive lynchpin and with Ferdinand's ban firmly in place, United finished the season in third.

He decided in May 2014 to bring the curtain down on his Manchester United career after 12 successful years at Old Trafford. A classy defender, Ferdinand made 455 appearances for the Reds, scoring eight goals. He won six Premier League titles, two League Cups, the Champions League and the FIFA Club World Cup.

He said upon leaving to join QPR: " I joined Manchester United in the hope of winning trophies, and never in my wildest dreams could I have imagined how successful we would be during my time here. "

He suffered a deep personal tragedy in early May 2015 when his 34 year-old wife Rebecca lost her battle against breast cancer. Premiership teams around the country wore black armbands out of respect to this hugely respected player. He also retired from playing in the summer of 2015.

Ferguson

With a stand named after him, and a statue outside the ground, there is no disputing that Sir Alex Ferguson is the greatest manager in the history of Manchester United – if not the history of football.

Not even his recommendation of the hapless David Moyes as his successor could stain his club CV after he won 38 trophies, including 13 Premier League titles and two Champions League titles, during his 26 years with the club.

After an unspectacular playing career as a centre forward including a spell at Rangers, Ferguson brought his skills and determination to football management.

He stayed at East Stirling for three months before being offered the managerial post at St Mirren where within 18 months he turned the team around and actively encouraged crowds to come and see his team play.

Ferguson then moved to Aberdeen where he broke the dominance of Celtic and Rangers in Scottish football, claiming three domestic League titles, four Scottish Cups, the European Cup Winners' Cup and a Scottish League Cup.

In November 1986, having been Scotland's caretaker manager for the World Cup in Mexico, he arrived at Old Trafford. His first few seasons proved difficult and he managed three unsuccessful campaigns before United won the FA Cup in 1990.

Ferguson realised that success had eluded the team simply because United had become used to Cup runs. With that in mind, he began to change his players and the departures involved Neil Webb, Jesper Olsen, Mark Robins and Paul McGrath, while newcomers included Steve Bruce, Gary Pallister, Peter Schmeichel, and Paul Ince.

Ferguson's second triumph was the European Cup Winners' Cup in 1991. Changes were also taking place

ABOVE Sir Alex Ferguson receives his manager of the month award, April 2008

in the youth system which was to grant significant results, but the most significant change of all was probably the arrival of Eric Cantona.

Criticised for his choice of player, Ferguson knew that Cantona was his lynchpin. His decision was proved right when United won the 1992-93 Premiership. This was followed by the Double in 1994 and domination of English football.

Fans were shocked by Ferguson's decision to sell Hughes, Kanchelskis and Ince, but he was confident in the youngsters coming through the ranks, who included David Beckham, Paul Scholes, and Ryan Giggs.

In 1999 Ferguson led his team to an unprecedented Treble by winning the Premiership, the FA Cup and the European Cup. The achievement saw Ferguson become the first working manager to be knighted for his services to the game.

He became the longest serving manager of Manchester United, overtaking Sir Matt Busby's record on 19 December 2010, and finally announced his retirement at the end of the 2012/13 Premier League season which, typically, he won!

Foulkes

For 18 seasons, Bill Foulkes (born 5 January 1932), was the rock at the heart of United's defence. He arrived at United in 1950, making his League debut against Liverpool in December 1952. He had convinced Matt Busby of his fitness for the game, although in fact he had an ankle injury which affected his appearances for the remainder of the season.

Playing at full-back, Foulkes was a regular member of the Busby Babes and was one of the survivors of the Munich air crash. Two weeks later, along with Harry Gregg, he was playing against Sheffield Wednesday in the fifth round of the FA Cup. Like Bobby Charlton, Foulkes was instrumental to Matt Busby's rebuilding of the United team and his manager put him in the centre-half position.

Bill Foulkes went on to score a spectacular goal in the semi-final of the 1968 European Cup against Real Madrid. His goal sent United to the Final, where the team beat Benfica 4-1. After Munich, it was an emotional time for those who had survived. United had rebuilt their shattered team and the consistent contributions made by Foulkes had been rewarded with European victory.

BELOW A stern Bill Foulkes

Giggs

ABOVE RIGHT Ryan Giggs tangles with Jason Roberts of Blackburn Rovers, 2008

A new chapter of the Ryan Giggs' story continued at Manchester United when he swapped his beloved number 11 shirt for a management suit at the start of the 2014-15 season.

Giggs finally called time on his playing career in order to work as new manager Louis van Gaal's assistant at Old Trafford with the promise that the new duo was ready to " make history ".

He played a record 963 times for the club, scoring 168 goals, having won 13 Premier Leagues, four FA Cups, four League Cups and two Champions League medals quite apart from the numerous times when the team finished runner-up in the various competitions.

The son of former Rugby League player Danny Giggs, he made his first appearance as a dashing left winger on March 2, 1991, aged just 17 and never left the first team for the next 23 years.

His most famous goal for the club came in the semi-finals of the FA Cup in 1999, when he punished a loose ball from Patrick Vieira, raced away from Lee Dixon, left Martin Keown for dead and fired past David Seaman as Tony Adams slid in despairingly.

Though his speed naturally waned in the latter part of his career, he was employed in a deeper playmaking role where his ability to hold the ball and create goal-scoring opportunities were the heartbeat of the team.

Giggs is the most decorated player in English football history and it is highly unlikely that anyone will ever match his trophies and awards. During his time at United, he was the first player in history to win two consecutive PFA Young Player of the Year awards (1992 & 1993), though he did not win the PFA Player of the Year Award until 2009.

He is the only player to have scored in every season of the Premier League and also holds the record for the most assists in Premier League history, with more than 270.

His international record of 64 caps, and 12 goals, could have been so much more if he hadn't of pulled out of so many internationals through injury – although the choice may not have always been his!

In addition to his many footballing

honours, he was appointed an OBE in the Queen's Birthday Honours List in 2007 and was named BBC Sports Personality of the Year in 2009.

Giggs was named Manchester United's greatest ever player by a worldwide poll conducted by United's official magazine and web-site; no one would bet against him eventually becoming one of their greatest ever managers.

ABOVE Giggs passes Peter Sweeney of Millwall during the 2004 FA Cup Final at the Millennium Stadium

Greatest XI

Manager

Sir Alex Ferguson

1	Peter Schmeichel
2	Gary Pallister
3	Bill Foulkes
4	Steve Bruce
5	Ryan Giggs
6	Bobby Charlton
7	Duncan Edwards
8	David Beckham
9	Denis Law
10	Eric Cantona
11	George Best

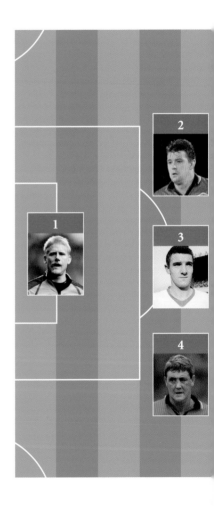

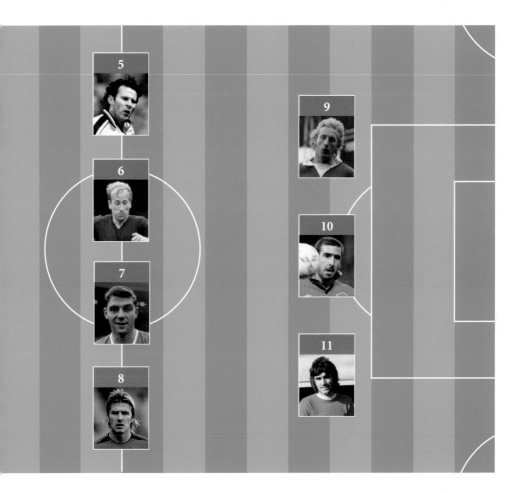

Greenhoff

Brothers Brian (born 28 April 1953) and Jimmy (born 19 June 1946) Greenhoff joined United in 1973 and 1976 respectively. Brian established himself as a midfielder while older brother Jimmy played in a forward position. Brian switched to centre-half after the 1974-75 season, playing alongside Martin Buchan in the FA Cup Finals of 1976 and 1977. He was rewarded for his efforts with England caps at full, 'B' and Under-23 levels.

Jimmy joined his younger brother at United from Stoke City when the club's flagging fortunes needed his inspiration. Despite being 30 when he signed in November 1976, he had impeccable ball control and the ability to score spectacular goals. He struck up a formidable partnership with fellow striker Stuart Pearson. During the 1977 FA Cup Final, Jimmy scored the winning goal against Liverpool, but found himself on the losing side in the Final two years later.

He left United in December 1980 and went on to join Crewe and Toronto Blizzard, making the last of his more than 650 League appearances in December 1983 with Rochdale.

Gregg

There are still older United supporters who will insist that even more than Peter Schmeichel or David de Gea it is Harry Gregg who warrants the accolade of the club's greatest ever goalkeeper!

Gregg dominated his box in an era when many 'keepers – including his predecessor at Old Trafford, Ray Wood – mainly stayed on their line. In an age when 'keepers received nothing like the protection they receive now, Harry would always be in the thick of action –even when that meant coming to the edge of his box to take a cross.

It took a world record fee for a goalkeeper of £23,500 to prise Harry from Doncaster Rovers in December 1957. Born in Derry on 25 October 1932, Gregg had begun with Linfield and Coleraine. Capped 25 times by his country, Gregg was named Goalkeeper of the Tournament at the 1958 when he helped Northern Ireland to the quarter finals of the FIFA World Cup

Harry played almost 250 games for Manchester United including the 1958 FA Cup final when he was knocked out in a 2-0 defeat to Bolton, but a recur-

ring shoulder injury cost him the chance to play more and he eventually moved on to Stoke in December 1966 but he only played twice for the Potters before commencing a decade in management with Shrewsbury, Swansea, Crewe and Carlisle.

Despite his prowess on the field of play the greatest of Harry's heroics came off the pitch. During the desperate trauma of the Munich air disaster in 1958 Gregg saved a woman and her baby by pulling them from the wreckage. Under two weeks later he was back in goal for United.

BELOW Harry Gregg (back row, fourth left) playing for Manchester United in Rotterdam September 1963

Herd

Just as George Harrison wasn't John Lennon or Paul McCartney, so David Herd wasn't Charlton, Law or Best, so perhaps at the time people didn't appreciate how good the Scottish international was, but 145 goals in 265 games illustrates that David was the real deal.

Bought from Arsenal for £37,000 in 1961 Herd led the line impressively and once partnered with Law a year later became even better. After scoring 17 goals in his first season Herd hit 21, 27, 28 and 33 in the following four campaigns before contributing 18 in 31 appearances as the title was lifted in 1966-67 during a campaign in which he broke his leg.

That leg break came as he scored against Leicester, a club against whom he netted 10 times in 11 games for United, two of those goals coming in the 1963 FA Cup final, which United won 3-1. Effectively that leg break ended Herd's time with United. He completed his career at Waterford playing for his old United team mate Shay Brennan, following a stint with Stoke.

David's father Alec; a Scotland war-time international, scored over 100 goals for Manchester City, and ended his career at Stockport – as a teammate of his son, Herd junior marking his debut with a goal against Hartlepool on the final day of the 1950-51 season.

Honours

LEAGUE CHAMPIONS

1907-08, 1910-11, 1951-52, 1955-56,
1956-57, 1964-65, 1966-67, 1992-93,
1993-94, 1995-96, 1996-97, 1998-99,
1999-2000, 2000-01, 2002-03, 2006-07,
2007-08, 2008-09, 2010-11, 2012-13

SECOND DIVISION CHAMPIONS

1935-36, 1974-75

FA CUP WINNERS

1908-09, 1947-48, 1962-63, 1976-77,
1982-83, 1984-85, 1989-90, 1993-94,
1995-96, 1998-99, 2003-04, 2015-16

FA CHARITY/COMMUNITY SHIELD

1908, 1911, 1952, 1956, 1957, 1965*,
1967*, 1977*, 1983, 1990*, 1993, 1994,
1996, 1997, 2003, 2007, 2008, 2010,
2011, 2013 (*shared), 2016

LEAGUE CUP WINNERS

1991-92, 2005-06, 2008-09, 2009-10,
2016-17

EUROPEAN CUP/ CHAMPIONS LEAGUE

1967-68, 1998-99, 2007-08

UEFA EUROPA LEAGUE

2016-17

EUROPEAN CUP WINNERS CUP

1990-91

UEFA SUPER CUP

1991

INTERCONTINENTAL CUP

1999

FIFA CLUB WORLD CUP

2008

FA YOUTH CUP WINNERS

1953, 1954, 1955, 1956, 1957, 1964,
1992, 1995, 2003, 2011

Hughes

Mark Hughes, born 1 November 1963, enjoyed two spells at United from 1983-86 and 1988-95. His flamboyant playing style delighted fans while his ability to win matches made him valued by his managers. He signed as a professional with United in November 1980 after five months as an apprentice. As a schoolboy player, United's youth coach Syd Owen changed his position from midfielder to centre-forward. He made his League Cup debut in November 1983 when Ron Atkinson gave the Welshman his first-team opportunity. During the 1984-85 season, Hughes was voted PFA Young Player of the Year.

In 1986, given the opportunity by Atkinson, he decided to sign for Barcelona, but his form suffered and he only managed one goal in 17 games. Hughes didn't settle in Spain and only scored four goals in 28 games. He was then loaned to Bayern Munich where he rekindled his love of football. Atkinson, who had not been forgiven for selling Hughes, was replaced by Alex Ferguson in 1986. Hughes was what Ferguson needed and he re-signed him for £1.5 million in 1988.

In 1989, 'Sparky' was voted Player of the Year, then in 1991 he became the first player to win the PFA Player of the Year award twice. He went on to win a second FA Cup winner's medal, the European Cup Winners' Cup against former team Barcelona and the League Cup. He formed a great alliance with Eric Cantona on his arrival in 1992 which helped United to their first League title for 26 years.

In January 1995, the arrival of Andy Cole marked the end of Hughes' time at United and he left for Chelsea for £1.5 million. He has since become an adept if not hugely successful manager with the Welsh national side, Blackburn Rovers, Manchester City, Fulham, QPR and Stoke, leading them to commendable top half Premier League finishes in 2013-15 seasons.

ABOVE Mark Hughes celebrates after scoring the third goal in the FA Cup Final against Chelsea in 1994

Ibrahimovic

RIGHT Zlatan scoring the 25,000th Premier League Goal while at Manchester United as drawn by graphic artist Mathew Vieira - www.mathewvieira.com

Zlatan Ibrahimovic needed to play for Manchester United. The Swedish superstar's CV was a stellar affair with entries including Barcelona, AC Milan, Juventus, Inter, PSG and Ajax since he started out in Sweden with Malmo- themselves former European Cup finalists.

Nominated for the FIFA Ballon d'Or an incredible nine times, Zlatan has too many Player of the Year and Goal of the Year awards to mention, as well as 28 trophies won before adding the Europa League, League Cup and Community Shield in his brief but unforgettable time at Old Trafford.

Just four months short of his 35th birthday when he signed in July 2016 Ibrahimovic's impact was immediate as he headed the winner in the Community Shield before marking his Premier League debut with a long-distance goal to help beat Bournemouth, swiftly followed up by both goals on his home debut against Southampton.

Always a headline waiting to happen, Zlatan registered the Premier League's 25,000th goal and soon added a European hat-trick – against St. Etienne – and a brace to win the League Cup final, again against the Saints.

Nominated for the PFA Player of the Year 'Ibra' was injured in the Europa League quarter-final and was reported to decline his wages whilst unavailable. After 28 goals in 46 games during his first season Zlatan agreed to a second year at the Theatre of Dreams but was restricted to just seven more appearances and a single goal before jetting off to add another chapter to his star spangled story with LA Galaxy.

Ince

Paul Ince, born 21 October 1967, provided United with its driving force in midfield during the early 1990s. He arrived in 1989 from West Ham United for £2 million. As a 21-year-old he had talent which was to develop over the six seasons he played for the club. His maturity enabled him to captain England, and he was the first black player to captain his country in a match against the United States, and he is only the fourth United player to captain an international game. In just one season he had gone from England debut to captain.

Partnered by Roy Keane in midfield, Ince maintained his tremendous form to be part of the team that won the Double in 1994. He had an incredible ability to run with the ball, setting up the attack for his team-mates, while his tackling skills frequently stopped the opposition. His departure from Old Trafford in June 1995 came as a shock, but Alex Ferguson thought that in his last season for the club Ince had underperformed. When Inter Milan offered a record £7 million for the player, his manager decided to let him go.

Ince has now turned his skills to managership and having cut his teeth

at Macclesfield went on to manage Blackburn Rovers before moving on to Milton Keynes Dons. His most recent appointments were with Notts County and Blackpool where his son also played for the first team.

ABOVE Paul Ince in action against Barcelona in the Champions League

OPPOSITE Mark
Jones, one of the
Busby Babes

BELOW Dennis Irwin
returns from training
at The Cliff

Irwin

Full back Denis Irwin was consistency personified as the Premier League and FA Cup double was achieved in 1993-94 and 1995-96. Composed and classy, Irwin made 529 appearances for United between the summers of 1990 and 2002. Bought from Oldham Athletic, the Latics were on the receiving end of three of his 33 goals, no club conceded more from Irwin in his time at Old Trafford.

As a defender his first priority was to defend, something he achieved with mastery. Going forward goals were a bonus but his ability to deliver precise curling crosses meant he constantly created the sort of havoc in opposition boxes that he helped to limit in United's.

Irwin's quality was illustrated by his ability to maintain his level at left back having spent his early years at United on the right, the flank he was naturally equipped for.

Finishing his career with Wolverhampton Wanderers Denis took his total of career games to an amazing 900 at club level; since his debut with Leeds, plus another 56 full internationals with the Republic of Ireland, two of those caps coming at the 1994 World Cup.

Jones

Mark Jones, born 15 June 1933, was just 17 when he made his United debut in 1950. Outside of football, Jones was renowned for his pipe-smoking and raising budgies which, alongside his impressive physical appearance, gave the impression of maturity beyond his years.

He joined the first team during the 1954-55 season, where as centre-half he created a formidable barrier for the opposition. He was renowned for keeping the ball on the move with simple but effective play and for passing the ball quickly. Matt Busby admired and valued his young player but Jones had to share his centre-half position with his friend and team-mate Jackie Blanchflower, whose skills were much in demand. Both players were products of the club's youth system.

Jones, one of the eight United players to be killed at Munich, was 24 when he died.

RIGHT Joe 'Jaws' Jordan

Jordan

Born in Scotland on 15 December 1951, Joe 'Jaws' Jordan intimidated opposing defenders with his direct and physical approach. Jordan was an international player for his country, gaining 52 caps. It was his winning goal that took Scotland to the World Cup Finals for the first time in 16 years in 1974.

After a successful career at Leeds, United signed him for more than £380,000 in 1978, a record fee at the time. As a strong and tall player, his skill and aerial ability made him a fearsome forward. In his time at Old Trafford he made 125 appearances and scored 41 goals. In 1981, Jordan left United to join AC Milan, before joining Verona. He later played for Southampton and Bristol City before taking up management positions at Bristol City, Heart of Midlothian and Celtic where he was assistant manager.

He had a long spell as coach at Portsmouth and when manager Harry Redknapp left to become manager of Tottenham Hotspur, he followed him to the club signing in November 2008.

Kanchelskis

Wide men tend to be speed merchants or jinky tricksters. Andrei Kanchelskis was both. Often it looked like Andrei was gliding on the skis that ended his name. A bargain buy from Shakhtyor Donetsk in 1991 Andrei's talent was exemplified by his stunning winner in the 1994 FA Cup semi-final replay with Oldham. Cutting inside from the right wing he worked his way across the edge of the box before curling home a shot with his weaker left foot from 20 yards.

The scorer of a hat-trick against Manchester City in November 1994 he would eventually achieve the feat of becoming the first man to net in Manchester, Merseyside and Glasgow derbies. He moved to Everton for the Toffees record fee of £5m after four years at United. During that time he scored 36 goals in 161 games and won the Premier League twice, as well as both domestic cups, the European Super Cup and the Charity Shield twice in addition to being the Sir Matt Busby Player of the Year in 1994-95.

Andrei would add half a dozen pieces of silverware later with Glasgow Rangers in a well-travelled career that also included spells in Italy, Saudi Arabia, Russia and a loan to Manchester City while at Ibrox, before a brief spell at Southampton.

Internationally he represented the Soviet Union and later Russia while in the transitional period in between he also played for what was called the CIS – Commonwealth of Independent States.

Since retiring from playing Kanchelskis has held managerial or administrative posts at five clubs in Russia, one in Latvia and from 2018 managed Navbahor Namangan in Uzbekistan.

ABOVE Andrei Kanchelskis celebrates scoring for United

Keane

OPPOSITE Roy Keane
during the Premier
League match between
United and Blackburn,
April 2005

Roy Keane dominated a football pitch as much as it is possible to do so. Beyond the fierce and famous competitiveness 'Keano' had the quality that combined with his commitment made him the best midfielder in the world at his peak.

First and fore-most Roy's football brain always kept him one step ahead. He didn't merely see situations and potential passes he had the technique to maximise what his radar brought to his attention. Add to that a will to win that was second to none, the ability to win the ball and a talent for scoring telling goals and Keane had it all.

Not one to suffer fools gladly, Roy expected and demanded the same standards he set himself from everyone else. Like a reformed smoker Roy relinquished the excesses of his youth to become the athlete's athlete. A devotee of green tea and the healthiest of lifestyles Keane came from Cobh Ramblers and having experienced the top class preparation being at United can afford expected the utmost in professionalism everywhere he went.

Never was this better illustrated than when he left the Republic of Ireland international squad ahead of the 2002 FIFA World Cup due to his dissatisfaction with his country's preparations. Regardless of the phenomenal furore that created Keane's aura was such that in years to come he took on a role as assistant manager of his country, teaming up with Martin O'Neill. The pair went on to link up again briefly at Nottingham Forest, the club both had played for under Brian Clough and who Roy left to join United for a British record fee of £3.75m in 1993.

Keane played 480 games in helping add the devil to the Red Devils but his fire was more often positive than punitive. The team always came first for the Cork-man. Never was this better seen than in the 1999 Champions League semi-final with Juventus. Despite a yellow card that meant reaching the final would be for the club but not himself it was Keane more than anyone who dragged United from the face of elimination to the elation of victory. Two down on aggregate in Turin, Keane refused to capitulate, halving the deficit when heading home a David Beckham corner. 'Keano' might as well have been playing against the 'Dog & Duck' rather than Zinedine Zidane, Edgar Davids, Antonio Conte and Didier Deschamps as he strode like an Emperor of all he surveyed, not resting until the tie was won.

Sir Alex described the performance as, "The most emphatic display of selflessness I have ever seen on a football field...he inspired all around him. I felt such an honour to be associated with such a player." Almost anyone would be delighted with such an accolade from the boss. Roy? "Stuff like that almost insults me. What am I supposed to do, give up...it's like praising the postman for delivering your letters. He's supposed to isn't he? That's his job." Truly there is only one Roy Keane.

Kidd

Born on 29 May 1949, Brian Kidd was a keen United supporter whose dreams came true when he signed schoolboy forms at the age of 14. He went on to sign apprentice forms before signing professionally for the team at the start of what was to be a fine career.

Kidd showed excellent form in United's reserve side and Matt Busby rewarded him with a debut at the start of the 1967-68 season in the Charity Shield when he went on as substitute for the injured David Herd. His impressive form ensured him of a regular first-team place – he only missed four matches during his first season.

On 29 May 1968, Kidd's 19th birthday, he played in United's European Cup Final victory over Benfica, scoring the third of United's four goals. As a tribute from fans, the Beatles classic 'Hello, Goodbye' was sung with the chorus words changed to "Eusebio, and I say Kiddo." Despite being capped for England twice, Kidd's only honour at United was that European Cup medal and he moved to Arsenal for £110,000 after United's relegation to the Second Division in 1974. His career was further enhanced by moves to Manchester City, Everton and Bolton Wanderers, before he rejoined Manchester United after spearheading the Professional Footballers' Association initiative to encourage clubs to work more closely with the community.

He eventually took over the youth development project and in 1991 became assistant manager to Alex Ferguson before an ill-fated sojourn as manager at Blackburn Rovers in the late 1990s. Varied backroom management positions have followed and Kidd became assistant manager to Roberto Mancini at Manchester City after Mark Hughes' sacking.

LEFT Martin Sullivan, CEO of AIG, poses with Ji-Sung Park (L), Wayne Rooney (2nd from left), Cristiano Ronaldo (2nd from right) and Gary Neville (R) after announcing the club's new shirt sponsors in 2006

Kits

Although everybody today associates Manchester United with red shirts, Newton Heath started their League career in shirts with red and white quarters and blue shorts. For ten years, they switched between this, white shirts and blue shorts and green and gold shirts. With chairman John Davies, came the red shirts that have now become a tradition. The basic red shirt did not dramatically change for years – although the club did experiment with a white shirt bearing a V around the neck and maroon shirts with white hoops during the 1920 and 1930s.

KITS

RIGHT Steve Bruce, models the 1992 away shirt

FAR RIGHT A group of shirts bearing the names and numbers of famous Manchester United players from the '90s

FAR RIGHT BOTTOM Bryan Robson in the 1990 away shirt

The shirts did not include an emblem on the chest until 1973, although badges were added for special occasions including FA Cup Finals. A badge depicting a phoenix rising from the ashes was added for the 1958 Cup Final held just three months after Munich. Replica kits were first made available to supporters in 1977 and sponsors' names appeared on the shirts in 1983.

From the start of the 2010-11 season, global insurance giant Aon became only the fourth sponsor in the club's history to see its name on Manchester United shirts.

In July 2012, United signed a seven-year deal with the American automotive corporation General Motors, which saw Aon replaced as the shirt sponsor from the 2014-15 season. United agreed a reported ten year £750m kit deal with Adidas in 2015.

Law

Combative Scot Denis Law's flair for being in the right place at the right time matched with his lightning football brain made 'the King' a prolific goalscorer over his 11 years at Old Trafford.

His early career saw him play for Aberdeen schoolboys, where his slim build and slight squint conspired against him, but this may also explain his aggressive style of play. As he was unable to wear his glasses on the pitch he played with his right eye shut. He soon attracted the attention of Archie Beattie, whose brother Andy was manager of Huddersfield Town where he was taken on as an apprentice in 1955. An operation cured his squint which gave him sight, though slightly blurred, in his right eye.

Matt Busby spotted Law (born 24 February 1940) in an FA Youth Cup tie against United and he offered Huddersfield £10,000 for him. The offer was rejected and Law went on to make his League debut for Huddersfield aged 16. Matt Busby, then manager of Scotland, capped Law against Wales in 1958 where he scored in a 3-0 win. After short spells for Manchester City and Torino, Law arrived at United in 1962. He quickly earned himself honours during the 1960s but missed out on the European Cup Final through injury.

Arriving at United for a British record transfer fee of £115,000. Denis lived up to the billing. The most clinical finisher, each of his goals would be signalled with a simple yet iconic celebration of one arm raised straight as a rod. That celebration came frequently. 160 of his goals came in his first 222 appearances – 46 of them in only 42

games in his second season as he set the club's seasonal goal-scoring record and was the winner of the Ballon' d'Or. During the same season he scored at Wembley for a 'Rest of the World' side against England.

With so many goals to his name it is easy but inaccurate to think of the Law-man as simply a supreme goal-poacher. Denis had so much more to his game. He was a terrific passer of the ball and unlike many a forward he could tackle too, and relished the opportunity.

At times his temper could be as red as his shirt and he was sent off three times in the sixties in an age when dismissals were much rarer than in the modern era.

At international level the last of his 55 caps for Scotland came in the 1974 FIFA World Cup. His tally of 30 goals for his country remains a record he holds jointly with Kenny Dalglish, although the latter played 47 more games than 'The King' to reach that total.

After 237 goals in 404 games for United, new manager Tommy Docherty believed Law had peaked and gave him a free transfer at the end of the 1972-73 season. He moved back to Manchester City and scored the goal that consigned United to the Second Division in 1974. He retired from football that year at the age of 34.

League Championship

United predecessors Newton Heath joined an expanded First Division in 1892 and endured a torrid two-year stay in the top flight, winning just six games out of 30 in each season, although they did register their record League victory, 10-1 against Wolves in October 1892. A 12-year spell in the Second Division ended in 1906 and United went on to enjoy a successful period for the rest of that decade. Mid-table mediocrity was then the norm until relegation in 1922.

The situation was dire on 5 May 1934 when United travelled to Millwall needing to win to avoid relegation to the Third Division (North) for the first time in their history. A 2-0 victory was achieved and two years later they clinched the Second Division title to claim a place in the top flight.

The club was a founding member of the Premier League in 1992, and after winning the Championship 13 times since its formation has now registered 20 League titles, a record for the English League.

ABOVE Sir Alex Ferguson and captain Roy Keane hold the Premiership trophy

ABOVE Alex Ferguson
leads out the team
to celebrate being
crowned FA Carling
Premier League
Champions, 2001

League Cup

Prior to facing Wigan in the 2006 Final, Manchester United had won the Football League Cup just once since its inaugural 1960-61 season. That was in 1992, when a Brian McClair goal beat Nottingham Forest 1-0 to claim the Rumbelows Cup (the trophy has also been known as the Worthington Cup, Milk Cup, Coca-Cola Cup and Carling Cup in its various incarnations).

It took them until 1982-83 to register their first appearance in the Final and their opponents were Liverpool, who were three-quarters of the way through a four-year domination of the competition. Although United took the lead through Norman Whiteside, Liverpool fought back to claim an extra-time victory. The Old Trafford side have been runners-up on two other occasions, losing to former manager Ron Atkinson's charges each time. In 1990-91 United registered their highest away win in the competition when they demolished Arsenal 6-2 at Highbury en route to a Wembley meeting with Sheffield Wednesday. The Owls managed just one shot on target during the whole 90 minutes and John Sheridan's strike proved decisive.

Three years later, United fell at the final hurdle to Aston Villa who took a 2-0 lead before Mark Hughes pulled one back with eight minutes remaining. Andrei Kanchelskis handled the ball in the last minute and Dean Saunders calmly stroked the ball past Les Sealey to seal a 3-1 win.

The 2006 Final victory over Wigan was something of a canter with two goals from Rooney and strikes from Saha and Ronaldo securing a 4-0 win, while they added the 2009 and 2010 League Cups to their trophy cabinet, after defeating Spurs and Aston Villa.

The trophy was won again in 2017 as Southampton were defeated 3-2 thanks largely to Man of the Match Zlatan Ibrahimovic's late winner, his second goal of the game.

ABOVE United players celebrate winning the Carling Cup after defeating Wigan Athletic in the Final at The Millenium Stadium, 2006

League Positions

Season	Division	P	W	D	L	F	A	P	Position
1892-93	Division 1	30	6	6	18	50	85	18	16th
1893-94	Division 1	30	6	2	22	36	72	14	16th
1894-95	Division 2	30	15	8	7	78	44	38	3rd
1895-96	Division 2	30	15	3	12	66	57	33	6th
1896-97	Division 2	30	17	5	8	56	34	39	2nd
1897-98	Division 2	30	16	6	8	64	35	38	4th
1898-99	Division 2	34	19	5	10	67	43	43	4th
1899-1900	Division 2	34	20	4	10	63	27	44	4th
1900-01	Division 2	34	14	4	16	42	38	32	10th
1901-02	Division 2	34	11	6	17	38	53	28	15th
1902-03	Division 2	34	15	8	11	53	38	38	5th
1903-04	Division 2	34	20	8	6	65	33	48	3rd
1904-05	Division 2	34	24	5	5	81	30	53	3rd
1905-06	Division 2	38	28	6	4	90	28	62	2nd
1906-07	Division 1	38	17	8	13	53	56	42	8th
1907-08	Division 1	38	23	6	9	81	48	52	1st
1908-09	Division 1	38	15	7	16	58	68	37	13th

Season	Division	P	W	D	L	F	A	P	Position
1909-10	Division 1	38	19	7	12	69	61	45	5th
1910-11	Division 1	38	22	8	8	72	40	52	1st
1911-12	Division 1	38	13	11	14	45	60	37	13th
1912-13	Division 1	38	19	8	11	69	43	46	4th
1913-14	Division 1	38	15	6	17	52	62	36	14th
1914-15	Division 1	38	9	12	17	46	62	30	18th
1919-20	Division 1	42	13	14	15	54	50	40	12th
1920-21	Division 1	42	15	10	17	64	68	40	13th
1921-22	Division 1	42	8	12	22	41	73	28	22nd
1922-23	Division 2	42	17	14	11	51	36	48	4th
1923-24	Division 2	42	13	14	15	52	44	40	14th
1924-25	Division 2	42	23	11	8	57	23	57	2nd
1925-26	Division 1	42	19	6	17	66	73	44	9th
1926-27	Division 1	42	13	14	15	52	64	40	15th
1927-28	Division 1	42	16	7	19	72	80	39	18th
1928-29	Division 1	42	14	13	15	66	76	41	12th
1929-30	Division 1	42	15	8	19	67	88	38	17th
1930-31	Division 1	42	7	8	27	53	115	22	22nd
1931-32	Division 2	42	17	8	17	71	72	42	12th
1932-33	Division 2	42	15	13	14	71	68	43	6th

LEAGUE POSITIONS

Season	Division	P	W	D	L	F	A	P	Position
1933-34	Division 2	42	14	6	22	59	85	34	20th
1934-35	Division 2	42	23	4	15	76	55	50	5th
1935-36	Division 2	42	22	12	8	85	43	56	1st
1936-37	Division 1	42	10	12	20	55	78	32	21st
1937-38	Division 2	42	22	9	11	82	50	53	2nd
1938-39	Division 1	42	11	16	15	57	65	38	14th
1946-47	Division 1	42	22	12	8	95	54	56	2nd
1947-48	Division 1	42	19	14	9	81	48	52	2nd
1948-49	Division 1	42	21	11	10	77	44	53	2nd
1949-50	Division 1	42	18	14	10	69	44	50	4th
1950-51	Division 1	42	24	8	10	74	40	56	2nd
1951-52	Division 1	42	23	11	8	95	52	57	1st
1952-53	Division 1	42	18	10	14	69	72	46	8th
1953-54	Division 1	42	18	12	12	73	58	48	4th
1954-55	Division 1	42	20	7	15	84	74	47	5th
1955-56	Division 1	42	25	10	7	83	51	60	1st
1956-57	Division 1	42	28	8	6	103	54	64	1st
1957-58	Division 1	42	16	11	15	85	75	43	9th
1958-59	Division 1	42	24	7	11	103	66	55	2nd
1959-60	Division 1	42	19	7	16	102	80	45	7th

Season	Division	P	W	D	L	F	A	P	Position
1960-61	Division 1	42	18	9	15	88	76	45	7th
1961-62	Division 1	42	15	9	18	72	75	39	15th
1962-63	Division 1	42	12	10	20	67	81	34	19th
1963-64	Division 1	42	23	7	12	90	62	53	2nd
1964-65	Division 1	42	26	9	7	89	39	61	1st
1965-66	Division 1	42	18	15	9	84	59	51	4th
1966-67	Division 1	42	24	12	6	84	45	60	1st
1967-68	Division 1	42	24	8	10	89	55	56	2nd
1968-69	Division 1	42	15	12	15	57	53	42	11th
1969-70	Division 1	42	14	17	11	66	61	45	8th
1970-71	Division 1	42	16	11	15	65	66	43	8th
1971-72	Division 1	42	19	10	13	69	61	48	8th
1972-73	Division 1	42	12	13	17	44	60	37	18th
1973-74	Division 1	42	10	12	20	38	48	32	21st
1974-75	Division 2	42	26	9	7	66	30	61	1st

Season	Division	P	W	D	L	F	A	P	Position
1975-76	Division 1	42	23	10	9	68	42	56	3rd
1976-77	Division 1	42	18	11	13	71	62	47	6th
1977-78	Division 1	42	16	10	16	67	63	42	10th
1978-79	Division 1	42	15	15	12	60	63	45	9th
1979-80	Division 1	42	24	10	8	65	35	58	2nd
1980-81	Division 1	42	15	18	9	51	36	48	8th
1981-82	Division 1	42	22	12	8	59	29	78	3rd
1982-83	Division 1	42	19	13	10	56	38	70	3rd
1983-84	Division 1	42	20	14	8	71	41	74	4th
1984-85	Division 1	42	22	10	10	77	47	76	4th
1985-86	Division 1	42	22	10	10	70	36	76	4th
1986-87	Division 1	42	14	14	14	52	45	56	11th
1987-88	Division 1	40	23	12	5	71	38	81	2nd
1988-89	Division 1	38	13	12	13	45	35	51	11th
1989-90	Division 1	38	13	9	16	46	47	48	13th
1990-91	Division 1	38	16	12	10	58	45	59	6th
1991-92	Division 1	42	21	15	6	63	33	78	2nd
1992-93	Premier League	42	24	12	6	67	31	84	1st
1993-94	Premier League	42	27	11	4	80	38	92	1st
1994-95	Premier League	42	26	10	6	77	28	88	2nd
1995-96	Premier League	38	25	7	6	73	35	82	1st
1996-97	Premier League	38	21	12	5	76	44	75	1st

Season	Division	P	W	D	L	F	A	P	Position
1997-98	Premier League	38	23	8	7	73	26	77	2nd
1998-99	Premier League	38	22	13	3	80	37	79	1st
1999-2000	Premier League	38	28	7	3	97	45	91	1st
2000-01	Premier League	38	24	8	6	79	31	80	1st
2001-02	Premier League	38	24	5	9	87	45	77	3rd
2002-03	Premier League	38	25	8	5	74	34	83	1st
2003-04	Premier League	38	23	6	9	64	35	75	3rd
2004-05	Premier League	38	22	11	5	58	26	77	3rd
2005-06	Premier League	38	25	8	5	72	34	83	2nd
2006-07	Premier League	38	28	5	5	83	27	89	1st
2007-08	Premier League	38	27	6	5	80	22	87	1st
2008-09	Premier League	38	28	6	4	68	24	90	1st
2009-10	Premier League	38	27	4	7	86	28	85	2nd
2010-11	Premier League	38	23	11	4	78	37	80	1st
2011-12	Premier League	38	28	5	5	89	33	89	2nd
2012-13	Premier League	38	28	5	5	86	43	89	1st
2013-14	Premier League	38	19	7	12	64	43	64	7th
2014-15	Premier League	38	20	10	8	62	37	70	4th
2015-16	Premier League	38	19	9	10	49	35	66	5th
2016-17	Premier League	38	18	15	5	54	29	69	6th
2017-18	Premier League	38	25	6	7	68	28	81	2nd
2018-19	Premier League	38	19	9	10	65	54	66	6th

BELOW United players
celebrate after Denis
Law scores his club's
third goal against
Arsenal to become
Division One Champions
at Old Trafford, 1965

League Title

Manchester United have won the Division One title on seven occasions, the first coming in 1907-08, only their second season back in the top flight, with a team including the inspira-tional Billy Meredith and Charlie Roberts. A further title followed in 1910-11 but the club would then have to wait 40 years before reclaiming the trophy.

The 1950s heralded a new era for the club with the introduction of the Busby Babes. Roger Byrne was the first of these youngsters to make his debut, in November 1951, and he contributed vital goals as United clinched the 1951-52 title. Back-to-back Championships were claimed between 1955 and 1957 when the likes of Bobby Charlton and Duncan Edwards swept all before them.

In 1955-56, Dennis Viollet scored 20 League goals as they lost just seven times, finishing 11 points clear of second placed Blackpool. The following year saw them win 28 games, losing just six times (three away and three home) but events in Munich tore the promising team apart. The final two titles of the pre-Premiership era arrived in the 1964-65 and 1966-67 with a side fronted by the awesome attacking force of Charlton, Law and Best.

Managers

The two managers that stand out and who have contributed more than any of the other 13 managers are Sir Matt Busby and Sir Alex Ferguson. Both tireless in their efforts to gain the best out of their respective teams, they each reaped the rewards of effort and determination with their personal best wins. For Matt Busby, winning the 1968 European Cup was a triumph, while for Alex Ferguson it is winning the Treble in 1999.

It all began with Ernest Mangnall's (1903-12) building of the new stadium at Old Trafford in 1910. He resigned from United and moved to Manchester City where he was again responsible for building a new stadium (Maine Road). Under his leadership United won promotion to the First Division in 1905-06 and won the FA Cup for the first time in 1909. Mangnall was replaced by John Robson in 1914 and despite World War I, Robson's team remained in the First Division but were relegated after his departure when he was succeeded by John Chapman in 1921.

Chapman endured a disappointing first season with United, but enjoyed promotion three years later when they went on to the FA Cup semi-finals, but were dashed by Mangnall's Manchester City. In 1926, due to misdemeanours that were never made public, Chapman was suspended by the FA and he made way for Clarence Hilditch (1926-27). As United's first ever player-manager, Hilditch's time at United was brief, returning to his playing role.

ABOVE Alex Ferguson watches from the bench during the Celtic v United Tom Boyd Testimonial at Celtic Park, May 2001

He was succeeded by Herbert Bamlett (1927-31), who had originally been a referee. His career as manager was not as successful as that of a referee and he was replaced by Walter Crickmer (1931-32), who never officially became manager, but took charge of team affairs twice during his 38-year career as secretary. In 1932, Scott Duncan began his five years at Old Trafford. Despite his experience as a player, Duncan never really made it as a manager and their position at the time was, and still is, United's lowest ever League position.

The club was without a manager until Matt Busby arrived in 1945. He was assisted by Jimmy Murphy who played an enormous part in rebuilding the team after the 1958 Munich disaster. Wilf McGuinness (1969-70) took over for six months following Matt

at both Chelsea and Queen's Park Rangers. Injuries to the team in 1980 caused poor results and Sexton's services were no longer required. Ron Atkinson took over in 1981, but again, due to poor form, the manager was replaced and Sir Alex Ferguson began his illustrious career with United in November 1986.

Sir Alex finally retired at the end of the 2012-13 season to be replaced by his recommendation as manager, David Moyes, who seemed out of his depth at a club of United's stature and was sacked in March 2014 following a disastrous season in which United finished seventh. Ryan Giggs took over the managership for a short while and although the choice of the fans to take over, former Dutch team manager Louis Van Gaal was appointed on May 19, 2014, under a three-year contract.

Van Gaal left after two seasons, signing off with a winning FA Cup final against Crystal Palace. In a gloriously trophy filled managerial career it proved to be Van Gaal's last match in football. He was replaced by Jose Mourinho who had 18 months and 144 games in charge before Ole Gunnar Solskjaer took over in December 2018.

Busby's retirement, but was quickly succeeded by Frank O'Farrell, the only Irishman to manage the club. He was dismissed after the team's bad form in the 1972-73 season.

Tommy Docherty (1972-77) was replaced by Dave Sexton (1977-81) who had previously replaced him

FAR LEFT Sir Matt Busby with the European Cup, July 1968

LEFT Van Gaal

Mata

Chelsea's loss was United's gain when Juan Mata – the best player at the London club – fell out of favour with manager Jose Mourinho and was transferred in the 2014 January window for a club-record fee of £37.1 million.

Some critics outside the club accused under-pressure manager David Moyes of paying over the odds for a big name player to appease the fans, but Mata soon proved his worth with fans voting him the player of the month for February 2014.

Although not blessed with blistering pace, or prone to tracking back, Mata exudes class, intelligence and panache and has superb vision to find a better placed player.

A graduate of Real Madrid's youth academy, he won the Copa del Rey in his debut season at Valencia and made over 170 appearances in four seasons before signing for Chelsea in August 2007.

He scored a goal on his debut against Norwich City and won the Champions League and the FA Cup in his first full season. He won the player of the year award two seasons' running and was being hailed as the next Zola before Mourinho's arrival signalled the end of his blue honeymoon.

Still only in his mid-20s, he is consistently an influential performer in any of the three main attacking positions across the pitch behind the lead striker – on either flank or in the no.10 role.

His game is about more than just attacking from deep to score goals. The Spanish international (he has more than 30 caps for his country) has a sweet left foot, wonderful poise and balance, and is a danger from set-pieces anywhere on the pitch.

His creativity sets him apart - only two players in Premier League history boast superior minutes-per-assist ratios – while his scissors kick volley away against Liverpool in March 2015 has written his name in United folklore.

McGuinness

Originally a Busby Babe, Wilf McGuinness's playing career was cut short when he broke his leg badly in a reserve match against Stoke City in 1960, forcing retirement at the age of 22. McGuiness, born 25 October 1937, became youth team manager in 1961 and became senior coach when Matt Busby announced his retirement in 1969.

A year later he was appointed manager but only held the post for six months. He returned to coaching the reserves for the following 12 months but then decided to take up a position as coach in Greek football to Aris Salonika and the Panachaiki Patras. He returned to England to manage York City, before spells with Hull City and Bury before retiring from football in 1992. He was a qualified physiotherapist and is currently an in-demand after-dinner speaker.

ABOVE Wilf McGuiness, pictured when a United player, went on to manage the club

McIlroy

Matt Busby's final signing in September 1969 was Samuel Baxter McIlroy, born 2 August 1954. The young player was a big United fan and George Best, a fellow Belfast lad, was his hero. McIlroy made a dramatic first-team debut for United three months after signing as a professional. The match was against Manchester City at Maine Road and he scored his first goal as a professional in front of a crowd of 63,000, having a hand in the other two in a thrilling 3-3 draw.

He was the third youngest player to be given an international cap, playing for Northern Ireland against Spain at the age of 17. After being seriously injured in a car crash in January 1973, he missed many games of the following season, but quickly established himself as a first team regular during 1973-74. Unfortunately, the team was relegated during that season but McIlroy bounced back with the side that won the Second Division Championship at the first attempt. By this time, he was also playing regularly for Northern Ireland, giving a resourceful performance as a midfielder while notch-

ing up an impressive goalscoring record.

He appeared in three FA Cup Finals for United and later collected a winner's medal when United defeated Liverpool at Wembley in 1977. In October 1981, he was dropped from the first team to make way for newly-signed Bryan Robson but he responded by scoring a hat-trick against Wolverhampton Wanderers. McIlroy made more than 400 appearances for United before being sold to Stoke City in 1982. He moved back to Manchester to join City three years later after a very short spell at Bury.

McIlroy clocked up 88 caps for Northern Ireland before he retired from playing. He subsequently managed several English football teams and the national team, gaining most success with Macclesfield Town. His last managerial position was at Football League Two side Morecambe before leaving in 2011.

Meredith

A giant of the game during the late 1890s and early 1900s, Billy Meredith joined United in 1906. As a slightly framed man, the Welshman, born 30 July 1874 and nicknamed 'Old Skinny', did not give the appearance of a footballer. However, his skills and his ability on the pitch gave him celebrity status long before being a celebrity was common.

He was renowned for playing with a toothpick sticking out of his mouth which he said helped him to concentrate – in fact, a newspaper cutting from 1909 claimed he was unable to play without it. Before joining United, Meredith was suspended in 1905 during his time at Manchester City for allegedly bribing an Aston Villa player. Meredith denied the charge but other financial irregularities were then found at Hyde Road and the FA dismissed several directors and banned several players for 12 months.

Although his ban was quashed in December 1906, Meredith had already been transferred to United and he played an instrumental part in turning them into one of the top clubs of the time. United won the League Championship in 1908 and 1911. In 1907, the Players' Union was formed. Meredith and other team-mates were under great pressure from the FA to disassociate themselves from the newly-formed body, but Meredith refused to conform and continued his association by joining several other United players and training independently for the 1909-10 season. They were known as 'The Outcasts'. Eventually the FA relented and an agreement was reached allowing the Union to be acknowledged. For Billy Meredith, this was one of his finest victories.

At the grand age of 47, Meredith retired from United after becoming increasingly disenchanted with the club. He re-signed for Manchester City as player and coach for a further three years, appearing in the FA Cup semi-final against Newcastle United at the age of 49.

BELOW Billy Meredith in action during the first ever FA Charity Shield match against Queens Park Rangers in 1908

Mitten

Born in Burma on 17 January 1921, Charlie Mitten joined United in 1936 and signed professional two years later, but he was to be with the club for nearly ten years before he made his full League debut. World War II began almost as soon as he signed and he worked as an RAF physical training instructor around Britain's aerodromes, but he was able to keep up his football and made guest appearances for clubs such as Chelsea and Tranmere Rovers.

In 1946, he made his debut for United under the guidance of Matt Busby, newly installed as manager. Occupying the left-wing position, Mitten was a pillar around whom Busby built his classic post-war side. Mitten's speed and shooting ability were an essential ingredient to success in the FA Cup triumph of 1948 and the following season his continued skill contributed to 23 goals in League and Cup games for the club.

In 1950 while touring in the US and Canada, several United players were approached by Colombian clubs, offering lucrative contracts. Mitten decided to go, and since Colombia was not a member of FIFA he was able to join Santa Fe FC, but within a year, his new nation had joined FIFA and he was obliged to return to an unforgiving Matt Busby. His decision cost him £250 and a six month suspension, whereupon he was transferred to Fulham for £20,000.

Mourinho

Mourinho's United win percentage of 58.33% has only been bettered by Sir Alex Ferguson (59.67%) in the history of the club.

The Europa League, League Cup and Community Shield were all won during Jose Mourinho's first season at Manchester United in 2016-17: Ajax, Southampton and Leicester being beaten as those trophies were secured.

After a promising second season in which 81 points also secured runners' up spot in the Premier League and United's highest points tally since their last league title in 2013, Mourinho's third campaign started disappointingly. This led to the Portuguese manager being dismissed a week before Christmas in 2018, following just seven wins from the opening 17 Premier League fixtures.

Unquestionably one of the biggest characters in the modern game, Mourinho won the Champions League with Porto and Inter, the Europa League with Porto and United and a total of eight league titles in Portugal, England, Italy and Spain, his three Premier League triumphs coming during his time with Chelsea, a club where he also

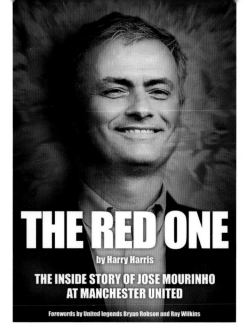

won the FA Cup and the League Cup twice.

At Real Madrid he won the Copa del Rey a year before lifting the La Liga title in 2011-12 but was unable to take them beyond the semi-finals of the Champions League, on one occasion losing to Bayern Munich on penalties.

The only coach to lead his side to league titles in La Liga, Serie A and the Premier League, Mourinho was sadly not quite the special one at Old Trafford but don't bet against him winning trophies at Tottenham, where he was appointed manager in November 2019.

ABOVE Mourinho's arrival at Manchester United was heralded by Harry Harris's biography The Red One - www.g2books.co.uk

Munich Air Disaster

The United players were on their way home from a European Cup quarter-final against Red Star Belgrade. On 6 February 1958, their plane stopped at Munich airport to refuel, a routine procedure that should have taken no longer than 20 minutes. What was to follow cost the lives of 21 people, including eight United players and three members of staff along with journalists, supporters and associates.

After a night of celebrations following the match in Belgrade, the Busby Babes boarded the Elizabethan class AS 57, 'The Lord Burghley', bound for home. The chartered plane was piloted by Captain James Thain and his friend and co-pilot Captain Kenneth Rayment. Captain Rayment was scheduled to pilot the plane even though Captain Thain was in command. As the plane reached Munich airport for the scheduled stop the passengers noticed it was snowing. As refuelling was not going to take long the passengers remained on board and at 2.31 pm with full tanks, Flight 609 received clearance to take off.

The plane picked up speed but the pilots could hear an odd note from the engines and take-off was aborted after 40 seconds. Both pilots agreed that the noise they heard was the result of 'boost-surging', caused by rich fuel making the engines over-accelerate. This was not uncommon in this type of plane and the pilots saw no reason for alarm. To compensate, the pilots let the throttle out more slowly and again attempted take off. The problem remained and the pilots decided to taxi back to the terminal and discuss what to do. The passengers were informed of a technical fault and asked to disembark.

While several passengers discussed the possibility of travelling overland or taking the Hook of Holland sea route, Duncan Edwards sent his landlady a telegram stating that he would be home the following day. He was wrong in his assumption that their flight was cancelled and the passengers were recalled. After consultation, the two captains had decided against an overnight stay in Munich in order to retune the engines and as the problem seemed confined to the port engine and the plane was able to take off with a single engine they were satisfied it was possible to leave the ground safely.

On its third attempt to leave the runway many of the passengers were frightened. Johnny Berry actually voiced his concern that they were all about to be killed, with devout Catholic Liam Whelan answering that he was ready to die. Just as the plane was about to take off it burst off the runway at high speed, skidding through a fence before it shot off across a road. After colliding with a house, which tore off a wing, the cockpit hit a tree while the body of the plane hit a hut full of tyres and fuel, causing the plane to explode with flames.

Harry Gregg became a hero by freeing himself from the wreckage and then rescuing a crying baby and her mother who had suffered a fractured skull and legs. He dragged Dennis Viollet and Bobby Charlton clear. By this time, Matt Busby was on the ground, while Jackie Blanchflower was lying badly injured. The stewardess was paralysed with shock. At last cars and trucks arrived at the crash scene. Passengers were rushed to the Rechts der Isar hospital in Munich. Matt Busby was to stay in hospital for 71 days, twice hav-

ABOVE An official from British European Airways' Munich office with firemen beside the wreckage of the BEA Elizabethan airliner

ing the last rites administered, before being allowed home to Manchester and Jimmy Murphy was left to pick up the pieces.

The eight players who died were: Geoff Bent, full-back (25); Roger Byrne, full-back (28); Eddie Colman, half-back (21); Duncan Edwards, half-back (22) – he survived for 15 days after the crash; Mark Jones, half-back (24); David Pegg, forward (22); Tommy Taylor, forward, (26) and Liam Whelan, forward (22), while the members of staff who perished include: Walter Crickmer, club secretary; Tom Curry, trainer and Bert Whalley, coach.

Neville

Gary Neville belongs to an elite group of players who have skippered the club to the Premier League title. Following on from Bryan Robson, Steve Bruce, Eric Cantona and Roy Keane, Neville realised a lifelong dream as he became the fifth United captain to lift the Premier League trophy following the club's record ninth triumph at the end of the 2006-07 campaign.

Neville himself had missed the final stages of the campaign, having suffered ankle ligament damage just 11 minutes into the visit of Bolton to Old Trafford on 17 March 2007. The same injury kept the Reds' skipper out for most of the 2007-08 season but even when unable to influence matters directly on the pitch, his presence is felt in the dressing room and from the stands. Nobody wants United to win more than Gary Neville.

The defender, who has made more than 560 appearances in a United shirt scoring seven goals since graduating from the youth team, was handed the armband during the 2005-06 season following Roy Keane's departure. Being one of United's most consistent and committed performers since establishing himself in the side in 1994-95 at the expense of Paul Parker, Neville was a natural choice and to this day he still enters every game refusing to contemplate defeat. Nobody wanted United to win more than Gary Neville.

Gary would give the club sterling service for nearly twenty years, racking up more than 600 first team appearances, of which 400 were in the League. That tally resulted in a haul of eight League titles, three FA Cups, two League Cups and the Champions League as well as 85 caps for England. He retired midway through the 2010-11 season and after chequered spells in coaching and management has found his calling as a top pundit with Sky Sports.

Newton Heath

Railway men from Piccadilly Station in Manchester formed a team made up of men from the carriage and wagon department of the Lancashire and Yorkshire Railway at Newton Heath. They formed the team, named Newton Heath LYR, in 1878 establishing themselves at a ground near the railway yard.

First games were often against other railway men and when the Football League was formed in 1888 the team did not think they were good enough to compete. Despite their lack of confidence, the team began to dominate local competitions and slowly began to look for games that could equal their talents. In 1890, Newton Heath applied to join the Football League, but without success, only gaining one vote. Undeterred, they formed an organisation called the Football Alliance and campaigned alongside other clubs to impress the Football League. After a further three applications they were eventually accepted in 1892.

The League had a reshuffle where the First Division was expanded, and included Newton Heath and the Second Division was born. Local rivals, Ardwick (later to become Manchester City), joined the Second Division. Newton Heath's career was neither exciting nor distinguished but after many and ups and downs, including times when the team was almost disbanded and debts totalled £2,600, Manchester United Football Club was born in 1902.

BELOW A Newton Heath fixture list from 1882-83

Nicknames

The giving of a nickname had a special status in Viking society in that it created a relationship between the name maker and the recipient of the nickname but Matt Busby was alleged to have disliked the term bestowed on his Busby Babes because he thought it cast aspersions on their youth. He preferred instead to label his youngsters the Red Devils. This term is now the club's nickname and is immediately identifiable all over the world.

The media was quick to label Alex Ferguson's crop of youngsters that dominated the Premiership in the 1990s Fergie's Fledglings. The stadium's nickname has also become synonymous with Manchester United after former hero Sir Bobby Charlton labelled Old Trafford the Theatre of Dreams.

It is not just the club, the ground or a set of players who have received nicknames over the years. Several individuals can be easily recognised by their alternatives. United have had two Kings (Denis Law and Eric Cantona) gracing the hallowed turf along with a Guv'nor (Paul Ince) and Captain Marvel (Bryan Robson), to name but a few.

Old Trafford

After the club won its first FA Cup in 1909, John Davies paid £60,000 for a site close to the Old Trafford cricket ground. The new stadium was designed by respected Scottish architect Archibald Leitch and was built with the likelihood of extension in mind.

Old Trafford's first match saw United play host to Liverpool on 19 February 1910 with VIP invitations boasting the new ground could accommodate 100,000 fans. A roof was erected over the United Road terrace in 1934 but bomb damage suffered during the Second World War prompted the redevelopment that began the creation of today's stadium.

United played their home games at neighbouring Maine Road while the ground was rebuilt. The Main Stand was covered in 1951 and the Stretford End in 1959 while March 1957 saw the floodlights turned on for the first time. The ground benefited from improvement in the mid-1960s to bring a 58,000-capacity in time for the 1966 World Cup. After the Taylor Report, the terraces disappeared from the Stretford End in 1993 with the away end soon suffering the same fate which reduced the capacity to 44,000. Between 1995 and 2000, capacity was increased to 68,000.

The stadium was chosen as a venue for the 1996 European Championships and hosted its first European Cup Final in 2003. Work has taken place to extend the capacity to approximately 76,000 by filling in the corners of the North East and North West corners and by adding an additional tier to link the North Stand with the East and Stretford Ends. Future expansion is likely to involve the addition of a second tier to the South Stand, which would raise the capacity to over 90,000.

ABOVE Inside Old Trafford, home of Manchester United

BELOW External view of Old Trafford

One Hundred Club

Player	Dates played	Goals
Wayne Rooney	2004-2017	253
Bobby Charlton	1956-73	249
Denis Law	1962-73	237
Jack Rowley	1937-55	211
Dennis Viollet	1952-62	179
George Best	1963-74	179
Ryan Giggs	1991-2014	168
Joe Spence	1919-33	168
Mark Hughes	1983-86, 1988-95	163
Paul Scholes	1994-2011, 2012-2014	155
Ruud van Nistelrooy	2001-2006	150
Stan Pearson	1937-54	148
David Herd	1961-68	145
Tommy Taylor	1953-58	131
Brian McClair	1987-98	127
Ole Gunnar Solskjaer	1996-2007	126
Andy Cole	1995-2001	121
Cristiano Ronaldo	2003-2009	118
Sandy Turnbull	1906-15	101
Joe Cassidy	1895-1902	100
George Wall	1906-15	100

Pallister

Beginning his career in non-League football with Billingham Town, Gary Pallister, born 30 June 1965, went on to become one of United's most successful players. Even when playing for Billingham, Pallister was working 16-hour shifts on Teesside Docks. In April 1988, while playing for Middlesbrough, he became one of the few players to be capped for England while playing outside the top division.

Signing for United in 1989, Pallister was a tall, commanding central defender who built a strong partnership with Steve Bruce. Their formidable alliance began on Pallister's signing and lasted until 1996, while between 1990 and 1992 their understanding for each other's game enabled them to win a hat-trick of Cup successes.

Pallister signed for the club for the record fee of £2.3 million and Alex Ferguson had high hopes for him. He recognised potential in Pallister and, after a shaky start where he conceded a penalty on his debut, put the mighty man on a rigorous training regime which built up muscle and turned Pallister at 6ft 4in into a giant. The triumphs and Cup victories gave United the chance and the confidence for a run of four Premiership titles in five years.

Missing only one game between 1992 and 1995, Pallister played over 400 times for United in all competitions, combining consistency with a fast pace and comfort with the ball. He received very few bookings during his career and was only once sent off which the FA later agreed was an error. During the 1995-96 season, he was forced to miss many games due to back problems, but managed to return for the climatic end to the season when United won their second Premiership and FA Cup Double.

Not known for his goalscoring, the two goals he headed into the net against Liverpool at Anfield undoubtedly won United the Premiership and Pallister received his fourth Premiership winners' medal. Back trouble again intervened and he finally moved back to Middlesbrough in July 1998 for £2.5 million.

BELOW Gary Pallister lifts the Premier League trophy after their 3-1 win over Blackburn Rovers at Old Trafford, May 1993

RIGHT David Pegg in action, February 1957

Pegg

It took diplomacy on the part of United's chief scout, Joe Armstrong to encourage David Pegg (born 20 September 1935) to sign for the club in 1952, aged 16. Pegg was the most sought-after schoolboy player, having earned five England schoolboy caps.

He was a naturally gifted winger who worked in real contrast to right-winger Johnny Berry. Berry was renowned for his direct approach and his ability to dart in and out of the opposition's territory, while Pegg was adept at swerving and fluid movement. But he also had the ability to cut inside suddenly and was most powerful close up with a left foot that could kick the ball with great force through the opposition defence.

He made his debut for United in December 1952 against Middlesbrough, but his position in the first team was not secure and he constantly battled with Albert Scanlon for the left-wing position. Matt Busby, had at the time, a team that was bursting with talent, but Pegg's performances in the FA Youth Cup saw victories in 1954 and 1956 and did much to enhance the image of the Busby Babes. David Pegg was a reserve at the time of the Munich air crash and sadly did not survive the tragedy.

Player of the Year

Awarded since 1974, members of the PFA, the players union, vote on who has been the best player. All professional footballers, regardless of nationality, under the age of 23 playing in the English leagues are eligible for the Young Player of the Year award and, the following Manchester United players have been recipients: Mark Hughes (1985), Lee Sharpe (1991), Ryan Giggs (1992 and 1993), David Beckham (1997),

ABOVE Cristiano Ronaldo was PFA Player (and Young Player) of the Year in 2007 and 2008

Wayne Rooney (2005 and 2006), Cristiano Ronaldo (2007). Recipients of the Player of the Year award are: Mark Hughes (1989 and 1991), Gary Pallister (1992), Eric Cantona (1994), Roy Keane (2000), Teddy Sheringham (2001), Ruud van Nistelrooy (2002), Cristiano Ronaldo (2007 and 2008), Ryan Giggs (2009) and Wayne Rooney (2010).

The Football Writers' Association have since 1948 presented an annual award to the player whom its members deem the best football player in England. The following United players have been honoured: Johnny Carey (1949), Bobby Charlton (1966), George Best (1968), Eric Cantona (1996), Roy Keane (2000), Teddy Sheringham (2001), Cristiano Ronaldo (2007 and 2008) and Wayne Rooney (2010).

Pogba

A World Cup winner with France in 2018, Paul Pogba was born on the outskirts of Paris on 15 March 1993 and first came to United in October 2009 having begun with a team called Torcy and then Le Havre.

An FA Youth Cup winner with United in 2011 he made his senior debut in a League Cup tie with Leeds in September of that year with a Premier League bow coming the following January, but there were just a handful of appearances before he switched to Juventus in the summer of 2012 after his contract expired.

Winning Serie A in four successive seasons from 2012-13 to 2015-16; during which time he also proved himself as a powerhouse in the midfield of the France international team, persuaded United to pay a world record fee of £89m to re-sign Pogba in August 2016.

The scorer of a brace in a notable derby victory over City towards the end of his second season back in Manchester, Pogba's prowess in the centre of the pitch is capable of making him as dominant as anyone worldwide, his strength, stamina and ability to pick out a pass and score from distance combine to make him the identikit box to box midfielder.

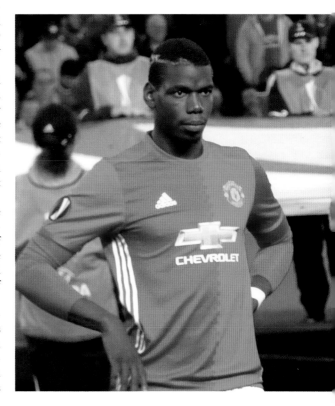

BELOW United's ebullient record signing Pogba in a calmer moment

Quixall

Albert Quixall was already the golden boy of English football when he crossed the Pennines from Sheffield Wednesday to join Matt Busby's bereft post-Munich team in September 1958. Busby paid a record British fee of £45,000 for the inside forward with an eye for goal.

Quixall was born in Sheffield on 9 August 1933 and turned pro with Wednesday in 1950. Blessed with sublime ball skills and a flair for invention, he rattled up 63 goals for Wednesday during an eight-year career at Hillsborough, and turned out five times for England.

He made his Old Trafford debut in a 2-2 draw with Tottenham Hotspur and, after a shaky start to the season, helped his new club finish as runners up in the First Division. He went on to make 184 appearances for United, ending his Reds career with 56 goals.

Fans lucky enough to have been in Munich in August 1959, when Bayern took on United in a pre-season friendly, witnessed a special Quixall moment: he scored from 58 yards, direct from the second-half kick-off, when he spotted the German goalkeeper off his line.

Quixall picked up an FA Cup winners' medal in 1963 before leaving the club for Oldham Athletic the following year, as a certain Denis Law arrived at Old Trafford. He subsequently played for Stockport County and Altrincham before retiring in 1968.

Rashford

Manchester born Marcus has been with United since he was seven. He became the youngest player to score on his England debut when he netted 138 seconds into his international career against Australia in May 2016 at the age of 18 years and 209 days. He swiftly became the youngest player at Euro 2016 a few weeks later – breaking Wayne Rooney's record of being England's youngest player at the Euros - before also appearing at the 2018 and 2022 FIFA World Cups.

First named on the bench by United in November 2015, three weeks after his 18th birthday, Rashford made his debut the following February, scoring twice in a Europa League match with Danish outfit Midtjylland – thus making an immediate mark by deleting George Best from the record books as United's youngest ever European scorer! Within three days Rashford had another brace to his name, this time in the Premier League (Becoming the club's third youngest Premier League scorer after Federico Macheda and Danny Welbeck).

Records and Rashford kept going hand in hand as at the age of 18 years and 141 days his winner in an away derby with City in March 2016 made him Manchester's youngest Premier League derby scorer.

Only Ryan Giggs reached a century of United league appearances at a younger age than Marcus who at the age of 21 signed a new four-year contact with his home town club in the summer of 2019.

ABOVE Marcus Rashford - United's next superstar

Roberts

Charlie Roberts, born 6 April 1883, became one of United's all time influential captains. Signing for the club in 1903, his transfer fee from Grimsby Town was £600. The meagre fee for such a phenomenal player was to turn out to be a great bargain for United and Roberts quickly became Ernest Mangnall's right-hand man on the field. He made his debut in 1904 and for the following nine seasons was rarely out of the first team. Playing in the centre-back position he established himself in the United defence.

Roberts, Dick Duckworth and Alex Bell contributed to one of the most outstanding half-back line-ups of all time. He captained a side that won League Championships in 1908 and 1911 as well

as taking United to lift the FA Cup for the first time in 1909. As a founding member of the Football Union, Roberts – alongside Billy Meredith – held strong in his principles and did not allow the FA to persuade him to renounce the newly formed Union.

Even though new clauses in players' contracts demanded that they renounce the Union, Roberts decided to fight, whereupon he was suspended by the FA. Like Meredith and several other United players, Roberts became one of 'The Outcasts' and began training independently for the 1909-10 season. When the FA were forced to reassess their position and players were allowed to return just hours before the beginning of the season, Roberts was able to go back to the job he did best, captaining the strong United side.

After nine years at United he was transferred to Oldham Athletic aged 30 and he went on to captain his new side to second place in the League Championship during the 1914-15 season. His fight for the Players' Union may have cost Roberts the opportunity of caps for England, as he gained only three, but Northern Ireland chose him to represent them nine times.

BELOW United captain Charlie Roberts before their match against Arsenal in 1912

OPPOSITE Bryan Robson celebrates another United victory

Robson

Captain of England 65 times, only Bobby Moore and Billy Wright have skippered the country more than 'Captain Marvel' as Bryan Robson became to be known. For nearly ten years, Robson led United and England, collecting 90 caps and six trophies. A win against Barcelona in the 1984 European Cup Winners' Cup quarter-final where he scored two goals showed him at his best.

Born on 11 January 1957, Robson started his career aged 15 with West Bromwich Albion. At 5ft 2in, weighing only 7 stone he was small, but according to his then manager Don Howe showed character and inner confidence. He was put on a diet of Guinness and raw eggs which helped to build him up and he made his professional debut for Albion in April 1975. In the following

season he played 16 times and the club won promotion. But Robson broke his leg three times during his first season and still managed eight goals in 23 appearances.

RIGHT RIGHT Bryan Robson at The Cliff, the club's old training ground

At Albion, Ron Atkinson was the manager under whom he worked best and the team went on to reach the UEFA Cup quarter-final beating Manchester United 5-3 at Old Trafford. After Atkinson moved to United, he managed to persuade Robson to join him so he could build a team around him to challenge Liverpool's domination. He made his debut for United at Tottenham in October 1981 four days after signing for the club for a record £1.5 million. He had made his debut for England a year earlier when they played the Republic of Ireland.

During 1982, while Kevin Keegan was out through injury, Robson became England's most influential player and Bobby Robson, the England manager (1982-90), was Robson's biggest fan, giving him the name of 'Captain Marvel'. Later that same year, Atkinson made him captain of United and he led the team to the 1983 FA Cup. In 1994 after several lean years with United, Robson was offered a coaching role at United but chose instead to …head into management with Middlesbrough, Bradford City, WBA, Sheffield United and from 2009-2011 the Thailand national team.

Ronaldo

ABOVE Cristiano Ronaldo - one of United's greatest ever players

The scorer of 118 goals in his 292 games for United between August 2003 and May 2005 (When he signed off in the Champions League final against Barcelona) Portuguese super-star Ronaldo was a thrill a minute player and has continued to remain so throughout his career.

In six years at Old Trafford, the Portuguese winger exhausted all superlatives as he matured from the inexperienced youngster who left Sporting Lisbon in 2003 to become arguably the best footballer on the planet.

The story goes that Sir Alex was persuaded to buy Ronaldo – largely unknown when he signed as an 18-year-old for £12.24 million in 2003 – by his players on the plane home from a pre-season friendly against Sporting. In his first season for the club, Ronaldo made 39 appearances and scored eight goals including one in the FA Cup Final against Millwall and was named the Sir Matt Busby Player of the Year.

On the international scene, he was one of the few Portuguese players who emerged from Euro 2004 with their reputation enhanced, while he survived an unseemly spat with clubmate Wayne Rooney in the following World Cup to become United's star of the 2006-07 season. That all paled into relative insignificance, however, compared with his achievements in the following campaign.

Taking the world by storm, Ronaldo scored 42 goals as United were supreme during 2007-08. His magical 2008 was rounded off with another string of individual honours. In October he was named Player of the Year, and in December became the first United player since George Best in 1968 to be awarded the prestigious Ballon d'Or trophy. To cap it off, in January 2009,

ABOVE Cristiano Ronaldo - one of United's greatest ever players

RONALDO

RIGHT Cristiano battles with Barcelona's Rafael Marquez during the UEFA Champions League semi-final, April 2008

he became the first Red to win the FIFA World Player of the Year award.

In his final appearance of the 2008-09 season at Old Trafford, Ronaldo received his third Championship medal after the Reds sealed the title with a point against Arsenal. At that stage, there was no indication that Cristiano was contemplating an exit – but that all changed less than a month later when the club announced it had accepted Real Madrid's world record £80 million offer.

The man from Madeira proved a bargain for Madrid. In nine seasons with Real Ronaldo played 438 times and astonishingly over such a long period scored a higher number of goals than he made appearances - 451 - making him Real's all-time top scorer! Consistency and class enabled him to average over a goal a game in both La Liga and European competition.

However, such was the competition from Barcelona and Lionel Messi that Ronaldo won fewer league titles in nine years with Madrid than he did in six at Old Trafford, three Premier League titles to two in La Liga. There was though the not inconsiderable achievement of inspiring Real to no fewer than four Champions League triumphs accompanied by three World Club Championship wins and a host of other silverware.

Moving on to Juventus in 2018 he added a Serie A title to his trophy cabinet in his first season in Italy. Internationally he led his country to success in the 2016 European Championships and inaugural Nations League title in 2019, while the number of individual awards Ronaldo has won is phenomenal – just as Cristiano has always been as a player.

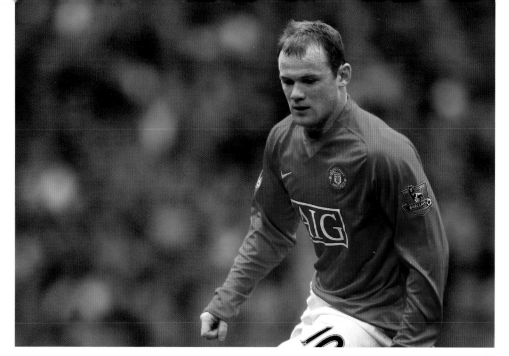

ABOVE Rooney in action in the Premier League, 2008

Rooney

Wayne Rooney joined United on 31 August 2004, transferring from Everton for a fee that could eventually reach £30 million. His League debut was against Spurs at Goodison Park at the start of the 2002-03 season, and nine games in he scored his first Premiership goal at the age of 16 in Everton's 2-1 victory over Arsenal.

With exceptional talents quickly spotted at international level, Rooney, born 24 October 1985, became England's youngest ever player in February 2003 when he was brought on as a substitute against Australia at Upton Park. He became the youngest player to score for his country when aged just 17 he netted a goal in September 2003 against Macedonia. He further impressed for England at the European Championships in

Portugal in 2004 where he scored four goals in four games, but his preparations for the 2006 World Cup were hampered by a broken metatarsal and his form didn't live up to expectations.

Sir Alex Ferguson had been watching Rooney since he was 14 and it was at this point that he decided he needed to sign the young striker, who made his debut for the club on 28 September 2004 against Fenerbahce. He scored twice in that match to endear himself to the United fans and would finish the season as the club's top scorer with 17 goals in all competitions.

By the end of his time with United – when he returned to his previous club Everton on a free transfer in 2017 – Rooney topped United's all time scorers' charts with a wonderful 253 goals from 559 appearances, a tally that included eight hat-tricks. After a season back at Goodison Park Rooney moved on to soccer in the USA with DC United before agreeing a deal to join Derby County in 2020.

Rowley

At the age of 17, in only his second appearance for United, Jack Rowley scored four goals in a League match against Swansea Town. Born 7 October 1920 in Wolverhampton, Rowley signed for United in 1937. As centre-forward, he proved he was a true professional having been spotted by Major Frank Buckley who never actually played him for the first team at Wolverhampton Wanderers.

He moved to Bournemouth and scored ten goals in his first 11 matches but was quickly signed by United who paid £3,000 for him. Like other players during World War II, Rowley missed around six seasons while on active service having joined the South Staffordshire Regiment. At the start of the war, League football was not played, but the government soon realised it was good for public morale and professional players then in service were actively encouraged to play for the League club they were nearest to.

Ironically, Rowley guested for Wolves and scored eight goals in the match, but making a guest appearance for

ABOVE Alf Ramsey (right) of Spurs tussles for the ball with Jack Rowley of Manchester United during their match at White Hart Lane, September 1953

Tottenham in 1944 proved memorable when he topped their goalscoring list and helped them win the League South title. He also played for England that same year and was given an assignment in the front line at the D-Day Normandy landings.

He returned to Old Trafford and became United's leading goalscorer during the 1945-46 season with 20 goals in 28 matches. During his 422 appearances for the club he scored 208 times. He moved to Plymouth Argyle in 1955 to become player-manager.

Schmeichel

Aged 20, Peter Schmeichel (born 18 December 1963), began his career at the Danish club of Hvidovre, where his talent was soon spotted by the Danish Premier side Brondby, who signed him in January 1987. At 6ft 4in, Schmeichel was a huge presence in goal and one of the tallest goalkeepers in League football. He was voted Danish Player of the Year in 1990 and became the best goalkeeper in European football. United were determined to sign him and Alex Ferguson got his man in August 1991 for the modest fee of £500,000.

In his first season he conceded only 33 goals in 42 League games which was the lowest number that season and, when United defeated Nottingham Forest at Wembley, Schmeichel received a League Cup winner's medal for the 1-0 victory. Schmeichel was happy at United and stated he would be with

the club 'for life'. The start to the 1992-93 season was not promising for Schmeichel who conceded six goals in the first three games, but he went on to keep five consecutive clean sheets between August and September. continuing to excel as he did so.

It was having Schmeichel in goal that enabled United to end their 26-year wait for the Championship and in February 1993 he was presented with the Premier League's Goalkeeper of the Year award. Only 31 goals made it past him in the entire season. During the following season, his ability to throw powerfully to the likes of Giggs and Sharpe and the fact he conceded very few goals allowed United to enjoy a Double-winning campaign. His penalty save from David Seaman against Arsenal in August ensured victory for United in the Charity Shield.

However, in the FA Cup quarter-final he was sent off and missed the League Cup Final defeat to Aston Villa. Up to his suspension, he managed to play in a total of 94 consecutive games which is the longest ever run for a United goalkeeper.

His goal was virtually untouched during the 1994-95 season but the following season was to show him at his best. In ten League games he only conceded seven goals which helped United to the Premiership title for the third time in four years. He enjoyed a fourth Championship medal at the end of the 1996-97 season when his outstanding contributions also included a save

from a header by Rene Wagner that already appeared to be in the goal. It turned the tables for United who were, by Schmeichel's actions, then able to secure a place in the quarter-final of the Champions League. In September 1995 he was voted European Goalkeeper of the Year.

He won a winner's medal with Denmark in Euro '96 and was voted Carling Player of the Year in August. Representing his country yet again in 1998, Denmark reached the quarter-final of the World Cup. Schmeichel, renowned for kicking both goalposts before a match for luck, decided to quit Old Trafford after the 1998-99 Treble.

ABOVE Schmeichel watches action during the FA Cup Final against Chelsea at Wembley, 1994

Scholes

Sir Bobby Charlton summed up Paul Scholes perfectly: "He was always so in control and pinpoint accurate with his passing – a beautiful player to watch."

Part of the new wave of talent that ushered in Beckham, Giggs, Butt and the Neville brothers in the mid-1990s, Salford-born Scholes scored twice on his debut in the League Cup at Port Vale in 1994/95 – and on his first league outing against Ipswich – and never looked back.

He went on to play a key part in the club's Treble-winning success in the 1998-99 season and has won 11 Premier League, three FA Cup and two Champions League winners medals.

The fiery red-headed midfielder also represented England from 1997 to 2004, gaining 66 caps and participating in the 1998 and 2002 World Cups as well as the Euros of 2000 and 2004.

Cited by many of his peers as one of the best footballers of his generation, his one weakness was his badly-timed tackling and he amassed more than 120 bookings, and ten sending-offs in his career – although was never a

particularly malicious player.

Scholes played 718 times for United, the third-highest number of appearances by any player for the club, and scored an impressive 155 goals – many of them spectacular efforts from outside the box.

He announced his retirement on May 31 2011, and following a testimonial match began his coaching career at the club from the 2011-12 season onwards.

However, manager Sir Alex Fergsuon, short of creative guile in midfield, persuaded him to come back and he went on to play one more fruitful season before retiring again in May 2013

At the end of the 2013-14 season, he assisted Ryan Giggs in taking charge of the first team following manager David Moyes's sudden departure. To the surprise of many the media shy Scholes moved into TV punditry and had a month long spell as manager of Oldham Athletic in 2019 having previously taken on a caretaker-manager role at Salford City, a club he is part-owner of.

BELOW Scholes nets for United against Sunderland

Solskjaer

Ole Gunnar Solskjaer's injury time winner in the 1999 European Cup final against Bayern Munich would have been sufficient to afford the Norwegian a place as a United legend, but the ability of the son of a champion wrestler to apply slide rule precision to his shooting made him much more than a one-game wonder.

Ole scored 126 goals in 366 games for United – many of those games being as a sub. It is a tally that includes four goals in an 11-minute spell in February 1999 and a best return of 25 goals in 47 appearances during 2001-02.

Having come to United from Molde, who he had joined from his first team Clausenengen FK, Solskjaer's early years at Old Trafford were punctuated by frequent speculation that he would move on in order to make more starts. It was even reported that

at the beginning of his Champions League winning season a £5.5m fee had been agreed for Ole to move to Spurs. Thankfully the player always preferred to stay with United where he spent the rest of his career, retiring through injury in 2007. The following year just under 69,000 attended his Testimonial against Espanyol with Ole appearing for the last 20 minutes of the match.

Beginning his coaching career with United, Solksjaer took over the reserve team in 2008 winning a couple of trophies before returning to his home country and old club Molde after leaving United in January 2011. After taking Molde to two league titles and the domestic cup he returned to British football after a three-year absence, taking over as manager of Cardiff City in January 2014. This was to be shortlived as following relegation Ole left the Blueburds in September 2014, taking over again at Molde just over a year later.

In December 2018 Solskjaer returned to Manchester United, initially as caretaker-manager, starting out with eight successive wins in all competitions and after winning six of the next nine he was confirmed as United manager on 28 March 2019.

BELOW Ole Gunner Solskjaer managing Manchester United in 2019

Stam

Jaap Stam was a top class defender who played for a host of top European clubs but despite impressing wherever he went it was only at United that he topped a century of appearances.

Arriving from PSV in July 1998 the Dutch international played 127 times before United made a handsome profit, moving him on to Lazio for over £15m after three years at Old Trafford. His purchase price of £10.6m had been both a Dutch record and also a world record for a defender.

During Stam's three seasons in England United were Premier League champions every year and also won the Champions League, the FA Cup and the Intercontinental cup. Having moved on to Italy Stam played for Milan as well as Lazio, reaching another Champions League final with the Rossoneri before completing his playing days back in the Netherlands with Ajax.

It was at Ajax that Stam served much of his 'apprenticeship' as a coach, being assistant there after an initial spell at PEC Zwolle where he had a stint as caretaker-manager. The summer of 2016 saw him

LEFT Jap Stam who manager Sir Alex Ferguson admitted he should never have let go

return to England in a managerial capacity with Reading but after leading the Royals to the Championship Play offs in his first season a bad run resulted in his dismissal. A return to PEC Zwolle as manager proved short-lived as he was soon approached by Feyenoord where he took over in the summer of 2019.

RIGHT Alex Stepney
pictured in September
1975

Stepney

RIGHT Alex Stepney pictured in September 1975

Alex Stepney was born 18 September 1942 and enjoyed a career at Old Trafford from 1966 to 1978. He became the top-scoring goalkeeper for the club when he converted two penalties in the 1973-74 season. Matt Busby was to say that "The single most important factor behind our Championship success in 1967 was signing Alex Stepney".

Not renowned for being a spectacular player, Stepney provided reliability and proved steady and efficient. His sense of anticipation and positioning was a rarity that was a bonus to the club. He was goalkeeper at a time when the club enjoyed enormous success, including the European Cup in 1968, where Stepney made an outstanding contribution by saving from Eusebio and United carried away the trophy, beating Benfica. Originally transferred from Chelsea for £55,000, Stepney, from south London, had already won three England Under-23 caps. He showed promise at a time when Matt Busby needed to strengthen his goalkeeping position.

Tommy Docherty, then manager of Chelsea, decided to let Stepney go after only five months with the club and he proved a key factor in United's League Championship of 1966-67, playing in every game. Chosen 20 times as a substitute for England, he only ever managed one full cap, against Sweden.

Stiles

Norbert 'Nobby' Stiles had no less than 28 England caps during his career. With United between 1960 and 1971, he won League Championship winner's medals in 1965 and 1967, and a World Cup winner's medal in 1966 followed by a European Cup winner's medal in 1968. In 14 years and nearly 400 appearances, Stiles, having signed for the club professionally in 1959, was thrown into first-team action making his debut in October 1960 against Bolton Wanderers.

Born 18 May 1942, Stiles had been an avid fan of United since a schoolboy and the local lad from Collyhurst established himself as a regular, making 31 appearances during his first season. His tackling was fierce and he was known for his aggressive style on the pitch which made him a permanent midfield fixture with the added bonus of being able to defend when necessary. His fitness levels were unique and he also hammered home goals when needed.

International recognition came for Stiles at the right time and in his first full-capped season he played no less than eight times, going on to figure in all England's World Cup matches. He will be remembered for his jig around Wembley when England celebrated victory against West Germany in a 4-2 win.

ABOVE Nobby Stiles pictured in December 1969

Stretford End

The Stretford End is where every Manchester United fan would like to sit to watch every home game. Situated opposite the Scoreboard End, the first cantilevered stand was built in 1964 at a cost of £350,000 but the current structure – completed almost 30 years later and boasting a 400-capacity banqueting suite – has a price tag of over £10 million. Since the changing rooms were built in 1993, the players emerge from the corner of the pitch by the Stretford End.

Supporters' Club

Supporters of United can be found worldwide. Although United have always enjoyed a 'big club' status in British football, it was the Munich air disaster that was to give the club its high profile throughout the world. It is the best-supported club in English football with huge attendances at home games while their away following is renowned for being one of the loudest in the country. The capacity of Old Trafford has just risen to 76,000, yet there are more than 140,000 members of the club.

There are 200 affiliated branches of the Manchester United Supporters' Club, the majority of which are UK based. United continues to enjoy strong support from Ireland with whom it has long had an affinity and small Irish towns regularly arrange travel to United games in England. One of the largest Supporters' clubs is based in Scandinavia, while other countries with branches include the US, Mauritius, South Africa and Iceland.

Taylor

One of the Busby Babes, Tommy Taylor (born 29 January 1932) signed for United in March 1953, making his debut at Old Trafford against Preston North End and scoring two goals. He was a talented youngster who had deputised for his uncle in a local pub team as centre-forward at the age of 16. He had started playing football some years earlier as left-back, playing only further forward when the school team was short of players.

He signed amateur forms at Barnsley in 1948, signing professionally for the club a year later. He made his debut in the first team in the Paisley Charity Football Cup in 1950 with his first League game against Grimsby later that same year. During national service, Taylor's football career was in jeopardy when he cracked a bone, tore ligaments and suffered severe cartilage damage. But a year out of the game and two operations later, Taylor was able to return to Barnsley.

Tommy opted to play for United rather than Cardiff City after 26 goals and 44 appearances for Barnsley when the Second Division team needed to sell him for financial reasons. United was not too far away from his Barnsley home and Taylor, described by Alfredo di Stefano as 'Magnifico', used his lightning speed, thunderous shots and powerful headers to become one of United's greatest goalscorers of all time.

After just ten weeks with United, Taylor was selected to tour South America for England, scoring in his international debut against Chile. Despite fierce competition, Taylor won a regular place on the team and in his last England game scored both goals in the 2-0 victory over France. He went on to score 25 goals in his 33 appearances for United during the 1955-56 campaign culminating in United winning the League.

In 1957, Tommy Taylor scored a hat-trick in the 10-0 victory over Belgian Champions Anderlecht, in United's first ever European Cup game. A year later, Taylor, along with seven other teammates, was killed at Munich.

BELOW Tommy Taylor, an international striker struck down in his prime

RIGHT Appearances in all competitions to end 2008-09 season

BELOW Ryan Giggs in action during the Premiership match between Chelsea and United at Stamford Bridge in April, 2006

Three Hundred Club

Player	Dates played	Appearances
Ryan Giggs	1991-2014	963
Bobby Charlton	1956-73	758
Paul Scholes	1994-2011, 2012-2014	718
Bill Foulkes	1952-70	688
Gary Neville	1992-2011	602
Wayne Rooney	2004 2017	559
Alex Stepney	1966-78	539
Tony Dunne	1960-73	535
Dennis Irwin	1990-03	529
Joe Spence	1919-33	510
Arthur Albiston	1974-88	485
Roy Keane	1993-05	480
Brian McClair	1987-98	471
George Best	1963-74	470
Mark Hughes	1983-86, 88-95	467
Michael Carrick	2006-2018	464
Bryan Robson	1981-94	461
Martin Buchan	1971-83	456
Rio Ferdinand	2002-2014	455
Jack Silcock	1919-34	449
Gary Pallister	1989-98	437
Jack Rowley	1937-55	424
Sammy McIlroy	1971-82	419
Steve Bruce	1987-96	414
Denis Law	1962-73	404
Lou Macari	1972-84	401
Peter Schmeichel	1991-99	398

Pat Crerand	1962-71	397
Steve Coppell	1975-83	396
Nobby Stiles	1960-71	395
David Beckham	1992-03	394
John O'Shea	1999-2011	393
Allenby Chilton	1939-55	391
Nicky Butt	1992-04	387
Phil Neville	1995-05	386
Patrice Evra	2006-2014	379
Mike Duxbury	1980-90	378
Gary Bailey	1978-86	375
Ole Gunnar Solskjaer	1996-07	366
Wes Brown	1996-2011	362
David De Gea	2011-2019	362
Mikael Silvestre	1999-08	361
Shay Brennan	1957-70	359
Johnny Carey	1937-53	344
Stan Pearson	1937-54	343
Darren Fletcher	2003-2015	342
Antonio Valencia	2009-2019	339
Billy Meredith	1906-21	335
David Sadler	1963-74	335
Charlie Moore	1919-30	328
Alfred Steward	1920-32	326
Chris Smalling	2010-2019	323
Clarence Hilditch	1919-32	322
George Wall	1905-15	319
Fred Erentz	1892-02	310
Alex Bell	1902-13	309
Charlie Roberts	1904-13	302
Ray Bennion	1927-32	301
Nemanja Vidic	2006-2014	300

BELOW Gary Neville during the Premiership match between Tottenham Hotspur and United at White Hart Lane in April, 2006

Treble

The 1998-99 season proved to be a momentous one for Manchester United with the club becoming the first to add the UEFA Champions League title (formerly the European Cup) to the domestic Double of Premier League and FA Cup.

The FA Cup run will forever be remembered for Ryan Giggs's solo goal which gave United victory over Arsenal in the semi-final replay. Hailed as the greatest-ever FA Cup goal, United were down to ten men following Roy Keane's dismissal when Giggs started his run in his own half and dribbled past five defenders before hammering the ball home. The Premiership title was wrapped up with a 2-1 victory at home to Spurs the week before the FA Cup Final. United's opponents at Wembley were Newcastle United, but goals from substitute and man of the match Teddy Sheringham and Paul Scholes sealed the Double.

In Barcelona four days later, United were trailing Bayern Munich to a Basler free-kick for most of the match. In injury time, Schmeichel came up for a corner and in the confusion Sheringham steered Giggs's mis-hit shot into the net for the equaliser. As the watching millions braced themselves for extra-time, United again won a corner. Ole Gunnar Solskjaer was the player to hit the back of the net this time and spark jubilant celebrations.

BELOW Manchester United celebrate winning the FA Premier League title after their victory over Tottenham on 16 May 1999

LEFT Alex Ferguson is held aloft by his team as they celebrate victory in the Champions League Final against Bayern Munich at the Nou Camp Stadium in Barcelona, 1999

UEFA Cup / Europa League

United won the Europa League in 2017, beating Ajax 2-0 in the Stockholm final with goals from Paul Pogba and Henrikh Mkhitaryan. The dreadful Manchester Arena bombing had occurred two days earlier. A minute's silence in respect of all those who suffered was held before the match.

United had never reached the Final of the UEFA Cup and they have suffered first-round exits on four occasions. Widzew Lodz went through on the away goals rule following a 1-1 draw at Old Trafford in 1980-81 while United lost 2-1 on aggregate against Valencia two years later. The opponents in 1992-93 were Torpedo Moscow and after two goalless games the Russians emerged victorious from the penalty shoot-out.

Rotor Volgograd were the visitors to Old Trafford in September 1995 and it took a headed Peter Schmeichel goal in the dying minutes to preserve United's unbeaten home record in Europe. The 2-2 draw was not enough to see United

progress, however, with Rotor claiming a second-round berth on the away goals rule. United did make it to the second round in 1976-77, losing 3-1 on aggregate to Juventus.

The 1984-85 season would take them closest to the trophy when they saw off the challenges of Raba Vasas, PSV Eindhoven and Dundee United on their way to a quarter-final meeting with Videoton. United won the home leg 1-0 but could not make a breakthrough in the second leg, conceding an equaliser in the first half. Extratime could not separate the sides and missed penalties by Frank Stapleton and Mark Hughes cost United a place in the semi-final.

RIGHT Eric Djemba-
Djemba battles Steve
Flack of Exeter City
during the FA Cup third
round match, 2005

Upsets

United have not been the victims of that many giantkillings in their time and it is the Cup competitions that provide the minnows with opportunity to ruffle a few feathers. In their first ever League Cup campaign in 1960, Third Division Bradford City ousted them from the competition with a 2-1 victory.

There were not many who would have predicted that Second Division York City would take a 3-0 first leg advantage away from Old Trafford and hang on to win 4-3 on aggregate in the 1995-96 League Cup second round. FA Cup upsets have come at the hands of Third Division Bristol Rovers (4-0 third round winners in 1955-56), Second Division Southampton (1-0 winners in the 1975-76 Final) and Third Division Bournemouth (2-0 third round winners in 1983-84).

Many also consider Exeter City's 0-0 draw with United in the third round of the 2004-05 FA Cup to be an upset. Fergie's team of youngsters could not break down the Conference side at Old Trafford, despite the introduction of Ronaldo, Scholes and Alan Smith

from the subs bench. United went on to win the replay 2-0 at St James' Park. A more recent shock was the pathetic showing at MK Dons when van Gaal's fledgling side lost 4-0 away in the Capital One Cup – a result that will always tarnish his MUFC CV.

Van der Sar

Since the departure of Peter Schmeichel in 1999, the goalposts at Old Trafford have seen nine different goalkeepers at a cost of £20 million. Of the most recent incumbents, Roy Carroll moved to West Ham in the summer of 2005, while Tim Howard did not prove reliable enough to be first choice.

Fabien Barthez was the most successful keeper for the longest time after Schmeichel's departure to Sporting Lisbon, but he was prone to high profile errors. Sir Alex Ferguson signed Edwin Van der Sar in June 2005 in a bid to solve what might have become a goalkeeping crisis. The move worked however, as Van der Sar shored up the back line and helped United to a hat-trick of Premier League titles as well as denying Anelka in the penalty shoot-out to win the Champions League Final.

Having played for Ajax and Juventus

and having made more than 150 appearances for Fulham, Van der Sar was in his mid thirties when he signed for the club but old father time had dulled neither his ambition nor his influence.

Edwin would go on to give United six seasons of sterling service, helping them win four Premier League titles, two League Cups and the Champions League. He retired at the end of the 2010-11 season at the age of 40.

ABOVE Kevin Campbell of West Bromwich Albion is halted by Edwin Van Der Sar

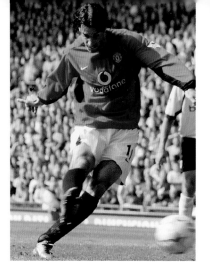

Van Nistelrooy

Born 1 July 1976, Ruud Van Nistelrooy's debut for United in August 2001 nearly did not take place after the striker found himself fighting to regain fitness after a knee injury threatened to rob him of his career. He was due to move from PSV Eindhoven and sign for United at the end of the 1999-2000 season, but the problem with his knee meant he had to return to Holland and undergo an extensive rehabilitation process. Once he had recovered he signed for the club for a transfer fee of £19 million and proved to Alex Ferguson and the rest of the team that he had been well worth the wait.

Teddy Sheringham and Andy Cole soon left and Van Nistelrooy became the exceptional striker that United were looking for. During the 2001-02 season he scored 36 goals and went on to set a new Premiership record by scoring in eight consecutive League games which included his first hat-trick for his team when they beat Southampton 6-1. His attitude was even more determined in his second season, scoring 44 goals with 15 of them coming in the last ten matches. But while the European Cup, the FA Cup and the League Cup eluded United, Van Nistelrooy's shooting ability ensured the club brought the Premiership trophy back to Old Trafford.

The start of the 2003-04 season saw him continuing his magnificent form and his goals in ten successive games beat the record of eight set by Liam Whelan in the 1950s. Van Nistelrooy helped United win the FA Cup in 2003-04 with two goals against Millwall in the Final. He had a contract with United that could have lasted at least until June 2008 but he was on his way to Real Madrid in the summer of 2006 after he fell out with Sir Alex.

Van Persie

Few Manchester United fans could have believed that their club would ever get their hands on Robin Van Persie. A key component of the Arsenal side for the best part of a decade, his exploits during the 2011-12 season marked him as one of the best strikers in the modern game.

Yet Manchester United received a glimmer of hope – Arsenal's lack of silverware prompted Robin to refuse to sign an extension to his contract, and with Arsenal facing the prospect of losing the player on a free transfer at the end of the 2012-13 campaign, opted to cash in whilst they could. There was to be fierce competition for the player, as might be expected, and whilst Arsenal might have preferred to sell him abroad, only Manchester United came anywhere near the valuation placed upon him. A £24 million deal therefore took him to Old Trafford in August 2012, where he instantly set about repaying the fee with a goal in his first full start and a hat trick at Southampton a week later.

By the end of his first season, United's no.20 was picking up his first title winners' medal having played a huge part in securing, rather aptly, title no.20 for the Reds.

ABOVE Van Persie in action for his national team

The Dutchman also claimed the league's Golden Boot after netting 26 times - he fired 30 goals overall, was voted the Sir Matt Busby Way Player of the Year and collected the Goal of Season accolade at United's annual awards dinner for his incredible volley against Aston Villa in April 2013.

Injuries, which blighted his entire career, limited his appearances for United although he scored more than a goal every other game - 58 in 105 appearances. He had a similar ratio at international level and was his country's all time top scorer with 50 goals in 102 matches.

Although his last boss at Old Trafford was also his former national team manager and family friend, Louis Van Gaal called time on RVP's spell at United - a fitting swan-song in the Premier League for a top player.

Vidic

There aren't many players who win half a dozen trophies in their first four seasons at a new club but that is exactly what Nemanja Vidic has achieved with three Premier League titles, Champions League and Fifa World Club Finals as well as a Carling Cup in 2009 and 2010.

Born in Yugoslavia on 21 October 1981, Vidic made his professional debut for Red Star Belgrade in 2000 and helped them to the League and Cup double in 2004 before signing for Spartak Moscow. Rated as one of the best defenders in Europe, he subsequently signed for United in 2005 for £7 million.

He formed an excellent partnership with Rio Ferdinand at the heart of the United defence, enabling the club to win five Premier Leagues, three League Cups and the Champions League during his time at Old Trafford. Having played 300 times for the Reds, he decided, somewhat surprisingly, to join Inter Milan on a free transfer in July 2014.

Viollet

A local lad born 20 September 1933, Dennis Viollet was an outstanding striker, particularly during the 1959-60 season when he scored 32 League goals. He signed for United in 1952, having joined Matt Busby's youth scheme after leaving school. He had a tremendous strength despite his slight frame that won him his first-team debut aged 19 alongside Tommy Taylor at Newcastle.

Like Taylor, Viollet won League Championship medals in 1956 and 1957. Renowned for his lightning runs, quick reflexes and intelligent positioning it was surprising he only won two caps for England, against Hungary and Luxembourg in 1960. Despite surviving the Munich air crash, he suffered head injuries which rendered him unable to play until the end of the 1957-58 season when he played as a warm up to the FA Cup Final against Bolton Wanderers. His form suffered for a time but was regained during the following season when his goals helped United finish second in the First Division.

He made 291 appearances in League and Cup competitions scoring a total of

ABOVE Local lad Dennis Viollet, a Munich survivor who served United well

LEFT Nemanja Vidic controls the ball

178 goals. He was forced to make way for Denis Law in 1962 and was transferred to Stoke City for £25,000. In more than 200 games he scored 66 goals before leaving in 1967 to play in the North American Soccer League for Baltimore Bays.

Viollet returned home after 18 months and continued to play football in Northern Ireland and for non-League Witton Albion. He coached at Preston and Crewe before returning to America. He returned to Munich in 1997 along with other survivors as a guest of UEFA to attend the European Cup Final.

Welbeck

Having worked his way through the ranks at United, Danny Welbeck established himself as a first-team regular and played an important role in helping the Reds scoop title no.20 in 2012-13.

The Manchester-born front man joined United's youth set-up in the summer of 2007 and quickly caught the eye with his skillful, strong and pacey displays.

He played sporadically for the first team while learning his craft but it wasn't until after a loan spell at Sunderland, where he scored six goals in 28 appearances, that he started to fulfill his potential.

The 2010-11 season also saw Welbeck made his senior international debut for England, as a substitute in a 1-1 friendly draw with Ghana, and he is now seen as an integral part of manager Roy Hodgson's plans.

In 2011-12, Welbeck came to the fore in the red shirt, scoring 12 times in 39 appearances in all competitions, including a contender for goal of the season against Everton, as he formed an eye-catching partnership with Wayne Rooney.

Welbeck's improved hold-up play, strength and finishing ability were rewarded with a nomination for the PFA Young Player of the Year award, and he went on to score England's winner against Sweden at the Euro 2012 finals in Kiev.

A new four-year contract followed in August 2012 with Welbeck going on to make 40 appearances during 2012-13 as the Reds stormed to title glory.

But football is a fickle master, and just as he looked set for a lengthy United career, Arsenal offered him more regular first team football and van Gaal let him go at the start of the 2014 season for a cut-price £16 million fee.

LEFT William 'Liam' Whelan, an Irish prodigy who perished at Munich

Whelan

Bert Whalley spotted William Whelan (born 1 April 1935) in 1953 playing with Home Farm FC, the famous Dublin nursery. Liam showed tremendous ball control and would leave opposition defenders stunned with sudden shots. His first match for United was in the 1953 FA Youth Cup Final which they won against Wolves, but he did not enjoy his first-team debut until March 1955.

Matt Busby was anxious about Whelan's lack of confidence. He was a modest player and unsure of his talents, but he won Championship medals in 1956 and 1957 and four caps for Ireland. He was United's leading League scorer in 1956-57 with 26 goals in 39 matches. Despite losing his position as inside-forward to Bobby Charlton, Whelan had travelled to Belgrade with the team in February 1958 and was killed at Munich.

ABOVE Norman Whiteside on the ball for United, 1985

Whiteside

Norman Whiteside is another Belfast lad to have made it to United. Born 7 May 1965, by the age of ten he had scored more than 100 goals in one season for his school. He went on to be the youngest player, aged 17, to score for United in a match against Stoke City. Sammy McIlroy declared he was "…a man well before his time. We used to joke that he was nine before he was born."

Whiteside was discovered by the same scout as George Best, Bob Bishop, who brought him to Old Trafford as a 13-year-old schoolboy in 1978. He signed professionally for the club in 1981, making his debut, aged just 16, in 1982 as a substitute for United at Brighton. By the age of 20, he had appeared in the World Cup Finals and was on the winning side of FA Cup victories on two occasions. His greatest moment came in the 1985 FA Cup Final when, deep into extra time, he charged down the pitch at Wembley and scored a stunning goal, from what many believed was an impossible angle, to win the Cup for United.

He was an extremely competitive footballer with a fiery temper, culminating in several suspensions and the press nickname of 'Nasty Norman'. Despite playing again in the 1986 World Cup Finals, Whiteside's form was suffering and he struggled with his fitness. He was sold to Everton in 1989 for £75,000, but a knee injury after two years forced early retirement at the age of 26. He left football in 1992 to pursue a career as a podiatrist.

World Club Championship

United's victories in the European Cup and Champions League (in 1968, 1999 and 2008) gained them entry to what was the Intercontinental Cup, now replaced by the World Club Championship. The first was a stormy two legged affair against Estudiantes of Argentina in 1968, with Estudiantes winning 2-1 on aggregate.

Fortunately, the introduction of a single match played in Tokyo resulted in better spectacles for the fans and, in 1999, a victory for United against Palmeiras with Roy Keane scoring the only goal. In 2008 United qualified for the semi final of the Wortld Club Championship, beating Gamba Osaka of Japan 5-3 to reach the final. There they faced LDU Quito of Ecuador in Yokohama and a 73rd minute goal from Wayne Rooney was enough to win the trophy for United, the only British winners of the competition.

ABOVE Dwight Yorke tussles with Amaral during the Vasco da Gama match in the World Club Championship, 2000

X-Tra Time

RIGHT Ruud van Nistelrooy celebrates scoring in the penalty shoot-out during the FA Cup Final against Arsenal, May 2005

Over the years, Manchester United have been involved in drawn Cup matches that have required replays to decide a winner but extra-time can provide a much more exciting finale. In 1887, however, Newton Heath were scratched from the FA Cup following their refusal to play extra-time after a 2-2 draw with Fleetwood Rangers.

When there is no possibility of a replay (becoming more and more common with the modern congested fixture list) and extra-time has been unable to provide a clear winner, the match has to be decided by a penalty shoot-out. United suffered in this manner for the first time in the FA Cup when they lost a second-round replay to Southampton in 1992-93. The 2004-05 FA Cup Final was also memorably decided in this fashion after United had dominated arch-rivals Arsenal during the game but had been unable to find the decisive strike.

Although not technically extra-time, injury time can play a major factor in the result as well. This is easily demonstrated in United's home Premiership clash with Sheffield Wednesday in April 1993. Trailing to a 64th-minute John Sheridan penalty, Steve Bruce popped up in the penalty area to head home the equaliser with four minutes left. It was Bruce who was again on target, heading in the winner six minutes and 12 seconds into injury time.

Young

Rejected by Watford as a youngster, Ashley Young battled back and made his name with...Watford! Born in Stevenage on 9 July 1985, Ashley had a brief spell at Watford's Academy before being released following an unsuccessful spell. Ashley worked at various aspects of his game and returned to the same club, this time getting accepted and rising through the ranks before making his first team debut in September 2003.

An eager and quick learner, Ashley would become an integral part of the young Watford side that defied the odds to not only survive in the Championship but ultimately gain promotion to the Premier League in 2006 through the play-offs. Whilst the step up a level would prove a difficult one for the club, there were several players who showed the elevated status held no fears, with Ashley Young head and shoulders above the rest. His performances attracted considerable interest from other clubs in the division, with Watford rejecting a number of offers during the course of the season. In January 2007, however, Aston Villa made an offer deemed acceptable and Ashley switch to Villa Park for a fee of £8 million plus add-ons.

Equally at home as a striker or attacking midfield player, Ashley quickly settled into the Aston Villa side and became an key figure for the club, earning selection for the PFA Premier League Team of the Year in 2008 and 2009 as wells as being named PFA Young Player of the Year in 2009. A desire to win club honours, however, soon meant Ashley was the target for other clubs, with Manchester United paying a reported £20 million in June 2011 to beat off competition from the likes of Liverpool.

Ashley made his United debt at Wembley in 2011 as Manchester City were defeated in the Community Shield. He subsequently helped win the Premier League in 2013 and the FA Cup three years later in addition to playing in the final of the same competition two years later.

Once a flying winger, the not so young Young developed his game as he got older playing in ever deeper positions for both United and England while still being a top performer. He retired from international football in 2018 after winning his 39th - and 24th with United - cap in July of that year in the World Cup semi-final against Croatia.

Youth Team

It was Matt Busby who pioneered the successful tradition of spotting talent in schoolboys and nurturing them. With the introduction of the FA Youth Cup in 1953 came United's domination of the early years of the competition as the Busby Babes went on to win it five times in succession.

Following their initial win, the team – including future stars Bobby Charlton and Duncan Edwards – was invited to attend the 1953-54 Blue Stars International Youth Tournament in Zurich. The next crop of youngsters to claim the title included George Best, David Sadler and John Aston Junior in 1963-64 and it would be another 18 years before a United youth team again graced the Final. Following Alex Ferguson's restructuring of the Old Trafford youth system, the trophy was brought back to Old Trafford in 1992, this time with a side including Nicky Butt, the Neville brothers, Paul Scholes, David Beckham and Ryan Giggs.

Two more wins followed in 1994-95 (a 4-2 penalty shoot-out win over Tottenham Hotspur after the aggregate scores were level at 1-1) and 2002-3 (a 3-1 aggregate win over Middlesbrough)

to leave United standing at the top of the pile with nine titles. In 2006-07 it was United's turn to lose out in a penalty shoot-out, Liverpool winning 4-3 after the two sides had drawn 2-2 over the two final matches. United's tenth (and so far last) victory in the competition came in 2010-11 when a 2-2 draw at Sheffield United was followed by a resounding 4-1 victory at home, with 23,000 being in attendance at Old Trafford to see the stars of tomorrow register a 6-3 aggregate win.

Zero

Goals may win matches, but any manager will tell you that even the best strike force in the game can be undone by a porous defence. Fortunately, United have been served by goalkeepers of exceptional quality, especially over the past couple of decades.

Peter Schmeichel made goalkeeping look easy, the result of his ability to marshal the forces in front of him to perfection, resulting in a peiord of some 694 minutes when United did not concede a single goal. That record was subsequently beaten by Petr Cech of Chelsea, but the record passed back into the safe hands of Edwin Van der Sar, who was not beaten for a total of 1,311 minutes, between Sami Nasri's strike for Arsenal on 8 November 2008 and Peter Lovenkrand's opener for Newcastle on 4 March 2009.

ABOVE Peter Schmeichel celebrates in May 1999

The pictures in this book were provided courtesy of the following:

GETTY IMAGES
101 Bayham Street, London NW1 0AG

PA PHOTOS
paphotos.com

WIKICOMMONS
commons.wikimedia.org

Design and artwork by Alex Young

Published by G2 Entertainment Limited

Publishers Jules Gammond and Edward Adams

Written by Jules Gammond

Updated by Rob Mason